GOOD
NEWS

THE
PSALMS

Today's English Version

PREFACE

The book of Psalms is the hymnbook and prayer book of the Bible. Composed by different authors over a long period of time, these hymns and prayers were collected and used by the people of Israel in their worship, and eventually this collection was included in their Holy Scriptures.

These religious poems are of many kinds: there are hymns of praise and worship of God; prayers for help, protection, and salvation; pleas for forgiveness; songs of thanksgiving for God's blessings; and petitions for the punishment of enemies. These prayers are personal and national; some portray the most intimate feelings of one person, while others represent the needs and feelings of all the people of God.

Many of the Psalms are quoted in the New Testament, and such passages as Mary's song of praise (Luke 1.46-55), Zechariah's prophecy (Luke 1.68-79), and Simeon's prayer of thanksgiving (Luke 2.29-32) reflect the language and style of the psalms. They were used by Jesus, quoted by the writers of the New Testament, and became the treasured book of worship of the Christian Church from its very beginning.

This translation of the Psalms attempts to represent the meaning of the Hebrew text as faithfully as possible, and at the same time convey something of the grace and beauty of the original poetry. The basic poetic structure of the Psalms consists of a statement which is repeated, in a modified fashion, in the next line. Sometimes this parallelism is continued over several lines. The possible variations are almost unlimited, and the reader who is aware of them will discover new beauty in the Psalms. In addition, unusual words and figurative expressions help create and sustain a poetic atmosphere.

Ancient Hebrew poetry did not have rhyme, and the meter was quite different from what is commonly used in English. This translation has been made in free verse, and the translators have tried to put the Psalms in easy-flowing, rhythmical lines that can be effective in public worship as well as in private devotion.

Like the New Testament in Today's English Version, this is a distinctly new translation that does not conform to traditional vocabulary or style, but seeks to express the meaning of the Hebrew text in words and forms accepted as standard by people everywhere who employ English as a means of communication. Where there is general agreement that the Hebrew text presents unresolved difficulties in interpretation, this translation employs the evidence of other ancient texts or follows present-day scholarly consensus. All such modifications are identified in footnotes.

This text was prepared by a committee working on a translation of the entire Old Testament. It was submitted to Bible scholars and stylists for study and comment, and was finally reviewed and approved by the Translations Committee of the American Bible Society. The line drawings were especially prepared to accompany the text.

THE PSALMS

BOOK ONE
(Psalms 1—41)

True Happiness

1 Happy is the man
who refuses the advice of evil men,
who does not follow the example of
sinners,
or join those who make fun of
God.
² Instead, he enjoys reading the law of the
Lord,
and studying it day and night.
³ He is like a tree that grows beside a
stream;
it gives fruit at the right time,
and its leaves do not dry up.
He succeeds in everything he does.

⁴ But evil men are not like this at all;
they are like straw that the wind blows
away.
⁵ Evil men will be condemned by God;
sinners will be kept apart from the righteous.
⁶ The Lord cares for the righteous man,
but the evil man will be lost forever.

God's Chosen King

2 Why do the nations plan rebellion?
Why do these people make useless
plots?
² Their kings revolt,
their rulers plot together
against the Lord and his chosen king.

³ "Let us free ourselves from their rule,"
      they say;
    "let us throw off their control."

⁴ From his throne in heaven the Lord
      laughs
    and makes fun of them.
⁵ He speaks to them in anger,
    and terrifies them with his fury.
⁶ "On Zion, my sacred hill," he says,
    "I have installed my king."

⁷ "I will announce what the Lord declared,"
      says the king.
    "The Lord said to me: 'You are my son;
    today I have become your father.
⁸ Ask, and I will give you all the nations;
    the whole earth will be yours.
⁹ You will rule over them with an iron hand;
    you will break them in pieces like a clay
      pot.' "

¹⁰ Now listen to me, you kings;
    pay attention, you rulers!
¹¹ Serve the Lord with fear;
    tremble ¹² and bow down to him;ᵃ
  or else he will be angry, and you will die,
    for his anger is quickly aroused.
  Happy are all who go to him for protec-
      tion!

Morning Prayer for Helpᵇ

3 I have so many enemies, Lord,
      so many who turn against me!
² They talk about me and say,
    "God will not help him!"

³ But you, Lord, always shield me from
      danger;

ᵃ*Hebrew unclear.* ᵇ*Hebrew title:* David wrote this psalm after he ran
away from his son Absalom.

you give me victory
and restore my courage.
⁴ I call to the Lord for help,
and from his sacred hill he answers me.

Always shield me from danger

⁵ I lie down and sleep,
and I wake up safe, because the Lord
protects me.
⁶ I am not afraid of the thousands of
enemies
who surround me on every side.

⁷ Come, Lord! Save me, my God!
You defeat all my enemies,
you destroy all the wicked.
⁸ Salvation comes from the Lord—
may he bless his people!

Evening Prayer for Help

4 Answer me when I call,
God, my defender!
When I was in trouble, you came to my
help.
Be kind to me now and hear my prayer!

² How long will you men insult me?
How long will you love what is worthless,
and go after what is false?

³ Remember that the Lord has chosen me
to be his own,
and hears me when I call to him.

⁴ Be afraid and stop your sinning;
think deeply about this,
alone and silent in your rooms.
⁵ Offer the right sacrifices to the Lord,
and put your trust in him.

⁶ There are many who say,
"How we wish to receive a blessing!"
Look on us with kindness, Lord!
⁷ The joy that you give me is much greater
than the joy of those who have plenty of
grain and wine.

⁸ As soon as I lie down, I go quietly to sleep;
you alone, Lord, keep me perfectly safe.

A Prayer for Protection

5 Listen to my words, Lord,
and hear my sighs.
² My king and my God,
listen to my cry for help.

I will pray to you, Lord;
³ in the morning you hear my voice;
at sunrise I offer up my prayer,
and wait for your answer.

⁴ You are not a God who is pleased with
wrongdoing;
you allow no evil in your presence.

⁵ You cannot stand the sight of proud men;
    you hate all wicked men.
⁶ You destroy all liars,
    and despise violent and deceitful men.

⁷ As for me, I can come into your house,
    because of your great love;
I can worship in your holy temple,
    and bow down to you in reverence.
⁸ Lord, I have many enemies;
    lead me to do your will,
    and make your way plain for me to
    follow!

⁹ What my enemies say can never be
    trusted;
    they only want to destroy;
their mouth is like an open grave,
    and their words are smooth and decep-
    tive.
¹⁰ Condemn and punish them, God;
    cause their evil plans to fail.
Throw them out of your presence
    because of their many sins
    and their rebellion against you.

¹¹ All who find safety in you will rejoice;
    they will always sing for joy.
You protect those who love you;
    because of you they are truly happy.
¹² You bless those who obey you, Lord;
    your kindness protects them like a
    shield.

A Prayer for Help in Time of Trouble

6 Lord, don't be angry and rebuke me!
    Don't punish me in your anger!
² Have pity on me, because I am worn out;
    restore me, because I am completely
    exhausted;

[3] my whole being is deeply troubled.
How long, Lord, will this last?

[4] Come and save me, Lord;
 because you love me, rescue me from
  death.
[5] In the world of the dead you are not
 remembered;
 no one can praise you there!

[6] I am worn out with grief;
 every night my bed is damp from my
  crying,
 my pillow is soaked with tears.
[7] My eyes are swollen from so much weeping,
 and I can hardly see—
 all because of my enemies!

[8] Go away, you evildoers!
The Lord hears my weeping;
[9] he listens to my cries for help,
 and answers my prayers.
[10] My enemies will all know the bitter shame
 of defeat;
 in utter confusion they will suddenly be
  driven away.

A Prayer for Justice[c]

7 Lord, my God, I have found safety with
 you;
 save me, and rescue me from all who
  pursue me,
[2] or else like a lion they will carry me off
 where no one can save me;
 and there they will tear me to pieces.

[3] Lord, my God, if I have done any of these:

---

[c]*Hebrew title:* A song which David sang to the Lord because of Cush
the Benjaminite.

if I have wronged someone,
4   if I have betrayed my friend,
     or without cause done violence to my
          enemy,
5 then may my enemies pursue me and
     catch me,
     may they cut me down and kill me,
     and leave me lifeless on the ground!

6 Rise in your anger, Lord,
     and stand up against the fury of my
          enemies!
  Wake up and help me,
     because justice is what you demand.
7 Bring together all the peoples round you,
     and rule over them from above.*d*
8 You, Lord, are the judge of all men.
     Judge in my favour,
     because I am innocent and good.

9 Stop the wickedness of evil men,
     and reward, I pray, the good men.
  You are a righteous God,
     and judge men's thoughts and desires.
10 God is my protector;
     he saves those who obey him.
11 God is a righteous judge
     and always condemns the wicked.

12 If men do not repent,
     God will sharpen his sword.
  He bends his bow and makes it ready;
13   he takes up his deadly weapons
     and aims his burning arrows.

14 See how the wicked man thinks up evil;
     he plans trouble and practises decep-
          tion.
15 He digs a deep hole in the ground,
     then falls into his own pit!

*d*rule over them from above; *Hebrew* return above over them.

¹⁶ So he is punished by his own evil;
he is hurt by his own violence.

¹⁷ I will thank the Lord for his justice,
I will sing praises to the Lord, the Most
High.

God's Glory and Man's Dignity

8 Lord, our Lord,
your greatness is seen in all the
world!
Your praise reaches up to the heavens;
² it is sung by children and babies.
You have built a fortress against your foes
to stop your enemies and adversaries.

³ When I look at the sky, which you have
made,
at the moon and the stars, which you set
in their places—
⁴ what is man, that you think of him;
mere man, that you care for him?

⁵ Yet you made him inferior only to your-
self;
you crowned him with glory and honour.
⁶ You made him ruler over all you have
made;
you placed him over all things:
⁷ sheep and cattle, and wild animals too;
⁸ the birds and the fish,
and all the creatures in the seas.

⁹ Lord, our Lord,
your greatness is seen in all the world!

Thanksgiving to God for His Justice

9 I will praise you, Lord, with all my
heart,
I will tell all the wonderful things you
have done.

Your greatness is seen in all the world!

² I will sing with joy because of you.
  I will sing praise to you, Most High!

³ My enemies turn back when you appear;
  they fall down and die.
⁴ As a righteous judge you sit on your
    throne,
  and you have judged in my favour.

⁵ You have condemned the heathen and
    destroyed the wicked,
  and they will be remembered no more.
⁶ Our enemies are finished forever;
  you have destroyed their cities,
  and they are completely forgotten.

⁷ But the Lord is king forever;
  he has set up his throne for judgment.
⁸ He rules the world with righteousness;
  he judges the people with justice.

⁹ The Lord is a refuge for the oppressed,
  a place of safety in times of trouble.
¹⁰ Those who know you, Lord, will trust you;

you do not abandon anyone who comes
     to you.

11 Sing praise to the Lord, who rules in Zion!
     Tell every nation what he has done!
12 God remembers those who suffer;
     he does not forget their cry,
     and he punishes those who wrong them.

13 Be merciful to me, Lord!.
     See how mistreated I am by those who
        hate me!
  Rescue me from death, Lord,
14   that I may stand before the people of
        Jerusalem
     and tell them all the things for which I
        praise you.
  I will rejoice because you saved me.

15 The heathen have dug a pit and fallen in;
     they have set a trap and been caught in
        it.
16 The Lord has revealed himself by his right-
        eous judgements,
     and the wicked are trapped by their
        own deeds.

17 Death is the destiny of all the wicked,
     of all those who reject God.
18 The needy will not always be neglected;
     the hope of the oppressed will not be
        crushed forever.

19 Come, Lord! Don't let men defy you!
     Bring the heathen before you and judge
        them.
20 Make them afraid, Lord;
     make them know that they are only
        men.

A Prayer for Help

10 Why are you so far away, Lord?
Why do you hide yourself in times
of trouble?

2 The wicked are proud and persecute the
poor;
may they be caught in the traps they
have made.

3 The wicked man brags about his evil
desires;
the greedy man curses and rejects the
Lord.
4 In his pride the wicked man says,
"God will not punish me! He doesn't
care!"
This is what the wicked man thinks.

5 He succeeds in all he does.
He cannot understand God's judgements;
he sneers at his enemies.
6 He says to himself, "I will never fail;
I will never be in trouble."
7 His speech is filled with curses, lies, and
threats;
he is quick to speak hateful and evil
words.

8 He hides himself in the villages;
he waits there and murders innocent
people.
He spies on his helpless victim;
9   he waits in his hiding place like a lion.
He lies in wait for his victim;
he catches him in his trap and drags him
away.

10 The helpless victim lies crushed;
brute strength has defeated him.
11 The wicked man says to himself, "God
doesn't care!

He has closed his eyes, and will never
    see me!"

¹² Come, Lord, and save me!
    Don't forget the oppressed, God!
¹³ How can the wicked man despise God,
    and say to himself, "He will not punish
    me"?

¹⁴ But you do see; you take notice of suffer-
    ing and grief
    and are always ready to help.
  The helpless man commits himself to you,
    because you have always helped the
    needy.

¹⁵ Break the power of wicked and evil men;
    punish them for their wickedness,
    until their punishment is complete.

¹⁶ The Lord is king forever and ever,
    and the heathen will disappear from his
    land.

¹⁷ You will listen, Lord, to the prayers of the
    lowly;
    you will give them courage.
¹⁸ You will hear the cries of the oppressed
    and the orphans
    and judge in their favour,
    so that mortal men may cause terror no
    more.

Confidence in the Lord

11 I trust in the Lord for safety.
        How foolish of you to say to me,
  "Fly away like a bird to the mountains,
²   because the wicked draw their bows
      and aim their arrows
    to shoot at good men in the darkness.

³ There is nothing a good man can do
  when things fall apart."

⁴ The Lord is in his holy temple;
  he has his throne in heaven.
He watches all men
  and knows what they do.
⁵ He examines both the good and the
  wicked;
  he hates the lawless with all his heart.

⁶ He sends down flaming coals*ᵉ* and burning
  sulphur on the wicked;
  he punishes them with a scorching
  flame.
⁷ The Lord is righteous and loves good
  deeds;
  those who obey him will live in his
  presence.

A Prayer for Help

12 Save me, Lord!
    There are no good men left,
  and honest men can no longer be found.
² All men lie to one another,
  and deceive each other with flattery.

³ Silence those flattering tongues, Lord,
  and close those boastful mouths!
⁴ They say, "We will speak as we wish,
  and no one will stop us.
  Who can tell us what to say?"

⁵ "But now I will come," says the Lord,
  "because the needy are oppressed,
  and the persecuted groan in pain.
  I will give them the security they long
  for!"

ᵉOne ancient translation coals; *Hebrew* traps.

⁶ The Lord's promises can be trusted;
    they are as genuine as silver,
    refined seven times in the furnace.

⁷ Keep us always safe, Lord,
    and preserve us from such people.
⁸ Wicked men are everywhere,
    and everyone praises what is evil.

A Prayer for Help

13 How long will you forget me, Lord?
    Forever?
    How much longer will you hide your-
    self from me?
² How long must I endure pain?ʃ
    How long will sorrow fill my heart day
    and night?
    How long will my enemies triumph
    over me?

³ Look at me, Lord my God, and answer
    me.
    Restore my strength, so that I will not
    die.
⁴ Then my enemies cannot say, "We have
    defeated him!"
    They cannot be glad over my downfall.

⁵ But I rely on your constant love;
    I will be glad, because you will save me.
⁶ I will sing to the Lord,
    because he has been good to me.

The Wickedness of Men
(Psalm 53)

14 Fools say to themselves,
    "God doesn't matter!"
They are all corrupt,

ʃOne ancient translation endure pain; Hebrew make plans.

they have done terrible things;
there is no one who does what is right.

2 The Lord looks down at men from heaven
to see if there are any who are wise,
any who worship him.
3 But they have all gone wrong,
they are all equally bad;
not one of them does what is right,
not a single one.

4 "Don't they know?" asks the Lord.
"Are all these evildoers ignorant?
They live by robbing my people
and do not pray to me."

5 But they will become terrified,
because God is with those who obey
him.
6 They make fun of the plans of the helpless
man,
because he trusts in the Lord.

7 How I pray that salvation
will come to Israel from Zion!
When the Lord makes his people prosperous again,
Jacob's descendants will be happy;
the people of Israel will be glad.

What God Requires

15 Lord, who may live in your temple?
Who may stay on Zion, your sacred hill?

2 The man who obeys God in everything,
and always does what is right;
whose words are true and sincere,
3   and who does not slander others.
He does no wrong to his friends
and does not spread rumours about his
neighbours.

⁴ He despises those whom God rejects,
  but honours those who obey the Lord.
He always does what he promises,
  no matter how much it may cost him.
⁵ He makes loans without charging interest
  and cannot be bribed to testify against
    the innocent.

He who does these things will never fail.

A Prayer of Confidence

16 Protect me, God, because I come to
    you for safety.
² I say to the Lord, "You are my Lord;
  all the good things I have come from
    you."

³ How excellent are the Lord's faithful peo-
    ple!ᵍ
  My greatest pleasure is to be with them.

⁴ Those who rush to other gods
  bring many troubles on themselves.ᵍ
I will not take part in their sacrifices;
  I will not worship their gods.

⁵ You, Lord, are all I have,
  and you give me all I need;
  my life is in your hands.
⁶ How wonderful are your gifts to me;
  how good they are!

⁷ I praise the Lord, because he guides me,
  and in the night my conscience warns
    me.
⁸ I am always aware of the Lord's presence;
  he is near, and nothing can shake me.

⁹ And so I am full of happiness and joy,
  and I always feel secure;

ᵍ*Hebrew unclear.*

¹⁰ because you will not allow me to go to the
world of the dead,
you will not abandon to the depths be-
low the one you love.

¹¹ You will show me the path that leads to
life;
your presence fills me with joy,
and your help brings pleasure forever.

The Prayer of an Innocent Man

17 Listen, Lord, to my righteous plea;
pay attention to my cry for help!
Listen to my prayer,
because there is no deceit in me.
² You will judge in my favour,
because you know what is right.

³ You know my heart;
you come to me at night.
You have examined me completely
and found no evil desire in me;
I speak no evil, ⁴as others do;
I have obeyed your command
and have not followed^h the path of violence.
⁵ I have always walked in your way
and have not strayed from it.

⁶ I pray to you, God, because you answer
me;
so turn to me and listen to my words.
⁷ Reveal your wonderful love, Saviour;
at your side we are safe from our enemies.

⁸ Protect me, as you would your very eyes;
hide me in the shadow of your wings
⁹ from the attacks of the wicked.

^h*One ancient translation* have not followed; *Hebrew* have followed.

My enemies, full of hate, surround me;
¹⁰   they have no pity and speak proudly.
¹¹ Now they are round me wherever I turn,
        watching for a chance to pull me down.
¹² They are like lions, wanting to tear me to
        pieces,
        like young lions, waiting for me in their
        hiding places.

¹³ Come, Lord, oppose my enemies and de-
        feat them!
Save me from the wicked by your sword;
¹⁴ save me from them by your power,
        from those who in this life have all they
        want.
Punish them with the sufferings you have
        stored up for them;
        may there be enough for their children,
        and some left over for their children's
        children!

¹⁵ Because I am righteous, I will see you,
        and when I awake, your presence will
        fill me with joy.

David's Song of Victoryⁱ
(2 Samuel 22.1–51)

18   How I love you, Lord!
            You are my defender.
² The Lord is my Saviour;
    he is my strong fortress.
My God is my protection,
    and I am safe with him.
He protects me like a shield;
    he defends me and keeps me safe.
³ I call to the Lord,
    and he saves me from my enemies.
Praise the Lord!

Hebrew title: These are the words that David, the Lord's servant,
sang to the Lord on the day the Lord saved him from Saul and all
his other enemies.

⁴ Death pulled its ropes tight round me;
    the waves of destruction rolled over me.
⁵ Death pulled its ropes tight round me,
    and the grave set its trap for me.

⁶ In my trouble I called to the Lord;
    I called to my God for help.
In his temple he heard my voice;
    my cry for help reached his ears.

⁷ Then the earth trembled and shook;
    the foundations of the mountains
      rocked and quivered,
    because God was angry!
⁸ Smoke poured out of his nostrils,
    a consuming flame and burning coals
      from his mouth.
⁹ He pulled back the sky and came down,
    with a dark cloud under his feet.
¹⁰ He flew down on the backs of the cherubim;
    he travelled swiftly on the wings of the
      wind.
¹¹ He covered himself with darkness;
    thick clouds, full of water, were round
      him.
¹² Hailstones and flaming coals
    came from the lightning before him
    and broke through the dark clouds.

¹³ Then the Lord thundered from the sky;
    and the voice of the Most High was
      heard.ʲ
¹⁴ He shot his arrows, and scattered his enemies;
    with flashes of lightning he sent them
      running.
¹⁵ The bottom of the ocean was revealed,

ʲ*One ancient translation (and see 2 Sam.22.14)* was heard; *Hebrew adds* hailstones and flaming coals.

and the foundations of the earth were
  uncovered,
when you rebuked your enemies, Lord,
  and roared at them in anger.

16 The Lord reached down from heaven and
    took hold of me;
  he pulled me out of the deep waters.
17 He rescued me from my powerful ene-
    mies,
  and from all those who hate me—
  they were too strong for me!
18 When I was in trouble they attacked me,
  but the Lord protected me.
19 He helped me out of danger;
  he saved me because he was pleased
    with me.

20 The Lord rewards me because I am right-
    eous;
  he blesses me because I am innocent.
21 I have obeyed the law of the Lord;
  I have not rebelled against my God.
22 I have observed all his laws;
  I have not disobeyed his commands.
23 He knows that I am faultless,
  that I have kept myself from evil.
24 And so he rewards me because I am right-
    eous,
  because he knows that I am innocent.

25 You, Lord, are faithful to those who are
    faithful,
  and completely good to those who are
    perfect.
26 You are pure to those who are pure,
  but hostile to those who are wicked.
27 You save those who are humble,
  but you humble those who are proud.

28 The Lord gives me light;
  my God dispels my darkness.

29 He gives me strength to attack my enemies,
      the power to overcome their defences.

30 This God—how perfect are his deeds,
      how dependable are his words!
   He is like a shield
      for all who seek his protection.

31 The Lord alone is God;
      God alone is our defence.
32 He is the God who makes me strong,
      who makes my pathway safe.
33 He makes me surefooted as a deer;
      he keeps me safe on the mountains.
34 He trains me for battle,
      so that I can use the strongest bow.

35 You, Lord, protect me and save me;
      your care has made me great,
      and your power has kept me safe.
36 You have kept me from being captured,
      and I have never fallen.
37 I chase my enemies and catch them;
      I do not stop until I defeat them.
38 I strike them down, and they cannot rise;
      they lie defeated at my feet.
39 You give me strength for the battle
      and victory over my enemies.
40 You make my enemies run from me;
      I destroy those who hate me.
41 They cry for help, but no one can save
them;
      they call to the Lord, but he does not
      answer.
42 I crush them, so that they become like
dust,
      which the wind blows away.
   I trample on them, like mud in the streets.

43 You save me from a rebellious people,
      and make me ruler over the nations;

people I did not know are now my subjects.

44 When they hear me they obey;
    foreigners bow before me.
45 They lose their courage
    and come trembling from their fortresses.

46 The Lord lives! Praise my defender!
    God is my Saviour! Proclaim his greatness!
47 He gives me victory over my enemies;
    he subdues the peoples under me
48   and saves me from my foes.

You, Lord, give me victory over my enemies
    and protect me from violent men.
49 And so I will praise you among the nations;
    I will sing praise to you.

50 God gives great victories to his king;
    he shows constant love to the one he has chosen,
    to David and his descendants forever.

God's Glory in Creation

19 How clearly the sky reveals God's glory!
    How plainly it shows what he has done!
2 Each day announces it to the following day;
    each night repeats it to the next.
3 No speech or words are used,
    no sound is heard;
4 yet their voice[k] goes out to all the world,
    their message reaches the ends of the earth.

[k]Some ancient translations voice; Hebrew line.

God set up a tent in the sky for the sun;
5   it comes out like a bridegroom striding
        from his house,
      like an athlete, eager to run a race.
6 It starts at one end of the sky
      and goes round to the other.
    Nothing can hide from its heat.

The Law of the Lord

7 The law of the Lord is perfect;
      it gives new life.
    The commands of the Lord are trust-
        worthy,
      giving wisdom to those who lack it.
8 The rules of the Lord are right,
      and those who obey them are happy.
    His commandments are completely just
      and give understanding to the mind.
9 The worship of the Lord is good;
      it will continue forever.
    The judgements of the Lord are just,
      they are always fair.
10 They are more desirable than gold,
      even the finest gold.
    They are sweeter than honey,
      even the purest honey.
11 They give knowledge to me, your servant;
      I am rewarded for obeying them.

12 No one can see his own errors;
      deliver me from hidden faults!
13 Keep me safe, also, from open sins;
      don't let them rule over me.
    Then I shall be perfect
      and free from terrible sin.

14 May my words and my thoughts be ac-
        ceptable to you,
      O Lord, my refuge and my redeemer!

A Prayer for Victory

20 May the Lord answer you in the day of trouble!
May the God of Jacob protect you!

[2] May he send you help from his temple
and give you aid from Mount Zion!

[3] May he accept all your offerings
and be pleased with all your sacrifices.

[4] May he give you what you desire
and make all your plans succeed.

[5] Then we will shout for joy over your victory
and celebrate your triumph by praising our God.
May the Lord answer all your requests!

[6] Now I know that the Lord gives victory to his chosen king;
he answers him from his holy heaven,
and by his great power makes him victorious.

[7] Some trust in their war chariots,
and others in their horses,
but we trust in the power of the Lord our God!

[8] They will stumble and fall,
but we will rise and stand firm!

[9] Give victory to the king, Lord;
the Lord will answer us when we call.

Praise for Victory

21 The king is glad, Lord, because you gave him strength;
he is full of joy, because you made him victorious.

[2] You have given him what he wanted;
you have answered his request.

[3] You came to him with great blessings
and set a gold crown on his head.

4 He asked for life, and you gave it;
  a long and lasting life.

5 His glory is great because of your help;
  you have given him fame and majesty.
6 Your blessings are upon him forever,
  and your presence fills him with glad-
    ness.

7 The king trusts in the Most High;
  and because of the Lord's constant love
  he will be king forever.
8 The king will catch all his enemies;
  he will capture all those who hate him.
9 He will destroy them like a blazing fire,
  when he appears.

The Lord will devour them in his anger,
  and fire will consume them.
10 The king will kill all their children;
  he will slaughter all their descendants.

11 They make evil plans and plot against
    him,
  but they will not succeed.
12 He will shoot his arrows at them,
  and make them turn and run.

13 Come, Lord, with your strength!
  We will sing and praise your power.

A Cry of Anguish and a Song of Praise

22 My God, my God, why have you
      abandoned me?
I have cried desperately for help,
  but it still does not come!
2 During the day I call to you, my God,
  but you do not answer;
I call at night,
  but get no rest.
3 But you are enthroned as the Holy One,
  the one whom Israel praises.

⁴ Our ancestors put their trust in you;
　　they trusted you, and you saved them.
⁵ They called to you and escaped from danger;
　　they trusted in you and were not disappointed.

⁶ But I am no longer a man; I am a worm,
　　despised and scorned by all!
⁷ All who see me make fun of me;
　　they stick out their tongues and shake
　　their heads.
⁸ "You relied on the Lord," they say. "Why
　　doesn't he save you?
　　If the Lord likes you, why doesn't he
　　help you?"

⁹ It was you who brought me safely through
　　birth,
　　and when I was a baby you kept me
　　safe.
¹⁰ I have relied on you ever since I was born;
　　since my birth you have been my God.
¹¹ Do not stay away from me!
　　Trouble is near,
　　and there is no one to help.

¹² Many enemies surround me like bulls;
　　they are all round me,
　　like fierce bulls from the land of Bashan.
¹³ They open their mouths like lions,
　　roaring and tearing at me.

¹⁴ My strength is gone,
　　gone like water spilled on the ground.
　All my bones are out of joint;
　　my heart feels like melted wax inside
　　me.
¹⁵ My throat*l* is as dry as dust,
　　and my tongue sticks to the roof of my
　　mouth.
　You have left me for dead in the dust.

*l*My throat: *Hebrew* My strength.

[16] A gang of evil men is round me;
   like a pack of dogs, they close in on me;
   they tear[m] my hands and feet.
[17] All my bones can be seen.
   My enemies look at me and stare;
[18]   they divide my clothes among them-
      selves
      and gamble for my robe.

Hurry and help me, my Saviour!

[19] Don't stay away from me, Lord!
   Hurry and help me, my Saviour!
[20] Save me from the sword;
   save my life from those dogs.
[21] Rescue me from those lions;
   I am helpless[n] before those wild bulls.

[22] I will tell my people what you have done;
   I will praise you in their meeting:
[23] "Praise him, you servants of the Lord!
   Honour him, you descendants of Jacob;
   worship him, you people of Israel!
[24] He does not neglect the poor or ignore
      their suffering;

[m]*Some ancient translations* they tear; *others* they tie: *Hebrew* like a lion. [n]*Some ancient translations* I am helpless; *Hebrew* you answered me.

he does not keep away from them,
    but answers when they call for help."

25 In the full assembly I will praise you for
        what you have done;
    in the presence of all who obey you
    I will offer the sacrifices I promised.
26 The poor will eat as much as they want;
    those who come to the Lord will praise
        him.
    May they prosper forever!

27 All nations will remember the Lord;
    from every part of the world they will
        turn to him;
    all races will worship him.
28 The Lord is king,
    and he rules over the nations.

29 All proud men will bow down to him;[o]
    all mortal men will bow down before
        him,
    all those who are bound to die.
30 Future generations will serve him;
    men will speak of the Lord to the com-
        ing generation.[p]

31 People not yet born will be told:
    "The Lord saved his people!"

The Lord Our Shepherd

23 The Lord is my shepherd;
        I have everything I need.
2 He lets me rest in fields of green grass
    and leads me to quiet pools of fresh
        water.
3 He gives me new strength.

---

[o]will bow down to him: *Hebrew* will eat and bow down. [p]*One ancient
translation* to the coming generation; *Hebrew* to the generation. They
will come.

He guides me in the right way,
as he has promised.
4 Even if that way goes through deepest
darkness,
I will not be afraid, Lord,
because you are with me!
Your shepherd's rod and staff keep me
safe.

5 You prepare a banquet for me,
where all my enemies can see me;
you welcome me by pouring ointment on
my head
and filling my cup to the brim.
6 Certainly your goodness and love will be
with me as long as I live;
and your house will be my home
forever.

The Great King

24 The world and all that is in it belong
to the Lord;
the earth and all who live on it are his.
2 He built it on the deep waters beneath the
earth
and laid its foundations in the ocean
depths.

3 Who has the right to go up the Lord's hill?
Who is allowed to enter his holy temple?
4 He who is pure in act and in thought,
who does not worship idols,
or make false promises.
5 The Lord will bless him;
God his Saviour will declare him innocent.
6 Such are the people who come to God,
who come into the presence of the God
of Jacob.

7 Fling wide the gates,
  open the ancient doors,
  and the great king will come in!
8 Who is this great king?
He is the Lord, strong and mighty,
  the Lord, victorious in battle!

9 Fling wide the gates,
  open the ancient doors,
  and the great king will come in!
10 Who is this great king?
The Lord of armies, he is the great king!

A Prayer for Guidance and Protection

25 To you, Lord, I offer my prayer;
    2 in you, my God, I trust.
Save me from the shame of defeat;
  don't let my enemies gloat over me!
3 Defeat does not come to those who trust
    in you,
    but to those who are quick to rebel
    against you.

4 Teach me your ways, Lord,
  make them known to me.
5 Teach me to live according to your truth,
  because you are my Saviour.
  All day long I trust in you.

6 Lord, remember your kindness and con-
    stant love,
  which you have shown from long ago.
7 Forgive the sins and errors of my youth.
Because of your constant love and good-
    ness,
  remember me, Lord!

8 The Lord is righteous and good;
  he teaches sinners the way they should
    go.
9 He leads the humble in the right way

and teaches them his will.
¹⁰ In love and faithfulness he leads
    all who obey his covenant and his com-
    mands.

¹¹ Keep your promise, Lord, and forgive my
        sins,
    because they are many.
¹² Those who obey the Lord
    will learn from him the way they should
        go.
¹³ They will always be prosperous,
    and their children will live safely in the
        land.
¹⁴ The Lord is the friend of those who obey
        him,
    and he teaches them his covenant.

¹⁵ I look to the Lord for help at all times,
    and he rescues me from danger.
¹⁶ Turn to me, Lord, and be merciful to me,
    because I am alone and weak.
¹⁷ Relieve me of all my worries
    and save me from all my troubles.
¹⁸ Consider all my distress and suffering
    and forgive all my sins.

¹⁹ Look at all the enemies I have;
    see how much they hate me!
²⁰ Protect me and save me;
    keep me from defeat,
    because I come to you for protection.
²¹ May my goodness and honesty preserve
        me,
    because I trust in you.

²² From all their troubles,
    save your people, God!

The Prayer of a Good Man

26 Declare that I am innocent, Lord,
      because I do what is right
and trust you completely.
2 Examine me and test me, Lord;
    judge my desires and thoughts.
3 Your constant love guides me;
    your faithfulness always leads me.

4 I do not keep company with worthless
      men;
    I have nothing to do with hypocrites.
5 I hate the company of evil men
    and avoid the wicked.

6 Lord, I wash my hands to show that I am
      innocent
    and march in worship round your altar.
7 I sing a hymn of thanksgiving
    and tell all your wonderful deeds.

8 Lord, I love the house where you live,
    the place where your glory dwells.
9 Do not destroy me with the sinners;
    spare me from the fate of murderers—
10 men who do evil at all times
    and are always ready to bribe.

11 As for me, I do what is right;
    be merciful to me and save me!

12 I am safe from all dangers;
    in public worship I praise the Lord!

A Prayer of Praise

27 The Lord is my light and my salva-
      tion;
    I will fear no one.

The Lord protects me from all danger;
   I will not be afraid.

2 When evil men attack me and try to kill
    me,
   they stumble and fall.
3 Even if a whole army surrounds me,
   I will not be afraid;
even if my enemies attack me,
   I will still trust God.

4 I have asked the Lord for one thing;
   one thing only do I want:
to live in the Lord's house all my life,
   to marvel at his goodness,
   and to ask his guidance there.

5 In times of trouble he will protect me in
    his shelter;
   he will keep me safe in his temple,
   and place me securely on a high rock.
6 So I will triumph over my enemies round
    me.
   With shouts of joy I will offer sacrifices
    in his temple;
   I will sing, I will praise the Lord!

7 Hear me, Lord, when I call to you!
   Be merciful and answer me!
8 "Come to me," you said.*q*
I will come to you, Lord;
9   don't hide yourself from me!·

Don't be angry with me;
   don't turn your servant away.
You have been my help;
   don't leave me, don't abandon me,
   God, my Saviour!

---

q "Come to me," you said; *Hebrew* I said to you, "Come to me" (you
is singular, Come *is plural*).

¹⁰ My father and mother may abandon me,
    but the Lord will take care of me.

¹¹ Teach me, Lord, what you want me to do
    and lead me along a safe path,
    because I have many enemies.
¹² Do not abandon me to my enemies,
    who attack me with lies and threats.

¹³ Certainly I will live to see
    the Lord's goodness to his people.
¹⁴ Trust in the Lord!
    Have faith, don't despair.
    Trust in the Lord!

A Prayer for Help

28 Lord, my defender, I call to you.
    Hear my cry!
If you do not answer me,
    I will be among those who go down to
    the land of the dead.
² Hear me when I cry to you for help,
    with my hands lifted towards your holy
    temple.
³ Do not condemn me with the wicked,
    with those who do evil—
men whose words are friendly,
    but whose hearts are filled with hate.

⁴ Punish them for what they have done,
    for all the evil they have committed.
Punish them for all their deeds;
    give them what they deserve!
⁵ They take no notice of what the Lord has
    done,
    or of what he has made;
so he will punish them
    and destroy them forever.

⁶ Give praise to the Lord;
    he has heard my cry for help!

7 The Lord protects and defends me;
    I trust in him.
He has helped me, and so I am glad
    and sing hymns of praise to him.

8 The Lord protects his people;
    he defends and saves his chosen king.
9 Save your people, Lord,
    and bless those who are yours!
Be their shepherd,
    and take care of them forever.

The Voice of the Lord in the Storm

29 Praise the Lord, you gods;
        praise his glory and power.
2 Praise the Lord's glorious name,
    bow down before the Holy One when
    he appears.

3 The Lord's voice is heard on the seas;
    the glorious God thunders,
    and his voice echoes over the ocean.
4 The Lord's voice is heard
    in all its might and majesty!

5 The Lord's voice breaks the cedars,
    even the cedars of Lebanon.
6 He causes the mountains of Lebanon to
        jump like calves,
    and Mount Hermon to leap like a young
        bull.

7 The Lord's voice makes the lightning
        flash.
8 His voice makes the desert shake;
    he shakes the desert of Kadesh.
9 The Lord's voice makes the deer give
        birth,
    and leaves the trees stripped bare,
    while in his temple all shout, "Glory to
        God!"

¹⁰ The Lord rules over the deep waters;
     he rules as king forever.
¹¹ The Lord gives strength to his people,
     and blesses them with peace.

A Prayer of Thanksgiving[r]

30   I praise you, Lord, because you have
         saved me
   and kept my enemies from gloating
     over me.
² I cried to you for help, Lord my God,
     and you healed me.
³ You brought me back from the world of
     the dead.
  I was with those who go down to the
     depths below,
     but you restored my life.
⁴ Sing praise to the Lord,
     his faithful people!
  Remember what the Holy One has done
     and give him thanks!
⁵ His anger lasts only a moment,
     his goodness for a lifetime.
  There may be tears during the night,
     but joy comes in the morning.

⁶ I felt secure, and said to myself,
     "I will never be defeated."
⁷ You are good to me, Lord;
     you have kept me safe as in a mountain
     fortress.
  But when you hid yourself from me,
     I was filled with fear.

⁸ I called to you, Lord;
     I begged for your help.
⁹ What good will come from my death?
     What profit from my going to the grave?
  Are dead people able to praise you?
     Can they proclaim your unfailing good-
     ness?

ʳHebrew title: A song for the dedication of the temple.

¹⁰ Hear me, Lord, and be merciful!
　　Help me, Lord!

¹¹ You have changed my sadness into a joy-
　　　ful dance;
　　you have taken off my clothes of
　　　mourning,
　　and given me clothes of joy.
¹² So I will not be silent;
　　I will sing praise to you.
　　Lord, you are my God,
　　　I will give thanks to you forever.

A Prayer of Trust in God

31　　I come to you, Lord, for protection;
　　　　never let me be defeated.
　　You are a righteous God;
　　　save me, I pray!
² Hear me! Save me now!
　　Be my refuge, to protect me;
　　my defence, to save me.

³ You are my refuge and defence;
　　guide me and lead me as you have
　　　promised.
⁴ Keep me safe from the trap that has been
　　　set for me;
　　you are my shelter.
⁵ I place myself in your care.
　　You will save me, Lord;
　　　you are a faithful God.

⁶ You hate those who worship false gods;
　　but I trust in you.
⁷ I will be glad and rejoice,
　　because of your constant love.
　　You see my suffering;
　　　you know my trouble.
⁸ You have not let my enemies capture me;
　　you have kept me safe.

⁹ Be merciful to me, Lord,
    because I am in trouble;
my eyes are tired from so much crying;
    I am completely worn out!
¹⁰ Sorrow has shortened my life,
    and weeping has reduced my years.
I am weak from all my troubles;*s*
    even my bones are wasting away.

¹¹ All my enemies make fun of me;
    my neighbours scorn*t* me;
those who know me are afraid of me;
    when they see me in the street, they run
        away.
¹² I am forgotten by all, as though I had died;
    I am like something thrown away.
¹³ I hear many enemies whispering;
    terror is all round me!
They are making plans against me,
    plotting to kill me.

¹⁴ But my trust is in you, Lord;
    you are my God.
¹⁵ I am always in your care;
    save me from my enemies
    and from those who persecute me.
¹⁶ I am your servant;
    look on me with kindness;
    save me because of your constant love!
¹⁷ I call to you, Lord;
    don't let me be defeated!
May the wicked be defeated;
    may they be silent in the world of the
        dead.
¹⁸ Silence those liars—
    all the proud and arrogant,
    who speak with contempt about right-
        eous men!

¹⁹ How wonderful are the good things

s Some ancient translations troubles; *Hebrew* iniquity. *t* scorn; *Hebrew*
exceedingly.

you keep for those who fear you!
How wonderful is what you do in the sight
    of everyone,
    protecting those who trust you.
20 You hide them in the safety of your pres-
    ence
    from the plots of men;
in a safe shelter you hide them
    from the insults of their enemies.

21 Praise the Lord!
How wonderfully he showed his love for
    me,
    when I was surrounded and attacked!
22 I was afraid, and thought
    that you had thrown me out of your
    presence.
But you heard my cry,
    when I called to you for help.

23 Love the Lord, all his faithful people!
The Lord protects the faithful,
    but harshly punishes the proud.
24 Be strong, be courageous,
    all who hope in the Lord!

Confession and Forgiveness

32 Happy is the man whose sins are for-
    given,
    whose transgressions are pardoned.
2 Happy is the man whom the Lord does
    not accuse of doing wrong,
    who is free from all deceit.

3 When I did not confess my sins,
    I was worn out from crying all day long.
4 Day and night you punished me, Lord;
    my strength was completely drained,
    as moisture is dried up by the summer
    heat.

⁵ Then I confessed my sins to you;
    I did not conceal my wrongdoings.
I decided to confess them to you,
    and you forgave all my transgressions.

⁶ So all your loyal people should pray to
    you in times of need;ᵘ
    when a great flood comes rushing, it will
    not reach them.
⁷ You are my hiding place;
    you will save me from trouble.
I sing aloud of your salvation,
    because you protect me.

⁸ The Lord says, "I will teach you the way
    you should go;
    I will instruct you and advise you.
⁹ Don't be stupid like a horse or a mule,
    which must be controlled with a bit and
    bridle,
    to make it obey you."

¹⁰ The wicked will have to suffer,
    but those who trust in the Lord
    are protected by his constant love.
¹¹ All who are righteous, be glad and rejoice,
    because of what the Lord has done!
All who obey him, shout for joy!

A Song of Praise

33 All you that are righteous,
    be glad because of what the Lord
    has done;
    praise him, all you that obey him!
² Give thanks to the Lord with the harp,
    sing to him with stringed instruments.
³ Sing a new song to him,
    play the harp with skill, and sing aloud!

ᵘ*Some ancient translations* need; *Hebrew* finding only.

4 The words of the Lord are true,
　　and all his works are dependable.
5 The Lord loves what is righteous and just;
　　his constant love fills the earth.

6 The Lord created the heavens by his com-
　　mand,
　　the sun, moon, and stars by his spoken
　　word.
7 He gathered all the seas into one place;
　　he shut up the ocean depths in store-
　　rooms.

8 Fear the Lord, all the earth!
　　Fear him, all peoples of the world!
9 When he spoke, the world was created;
　　at his command everything appeared.

10 The Lord frustrates the purposes of the
　　nations;
　　he keeps them from carrying out their
　　plans.
11 But his plans endure forever,
　　his purposes last eternally.
12 Happy is the nation whose God is the
　　Lord;
　　happy are the people he has chosen for
　　his own!

13 The Lord looks down from heaven
　　and sees all mankind.
14 From where he rules he looks down
　　on all who live on earth.
15 He forms all their thoughts,
　　and knows everything they do.

16 A king does not win because of his power-
　　ful army;
　　a soldier does not triumph because of
　　his strength.
17 War horses are useless for victory;
　　their great strength cannot save.

18 The Lord watches over those who fear
     him,
     those who trust in his constant love.
19 He saves them from death;
     he keeps them alive in times of famine.

20 We put our hope in the Lord;
     he is our helper and protector.
21 We are glad because of him;
     we trust in his holy name.

22 May your constant love be with us, Lord,
     as we put our hope in you.

In Praise of God's Goodness[v]

34 I will always thank the Lord;
     I will never stop praising him.
2 I will praise him for what he has done;
     may all who are oppressed listen and be
          glad!
3 Proclaim with me the Lord's greatness;
     let us praise his name together!

4 I prayed to the Lord and he answered me;
     he freed me from all my fears.
5 The oppressed look to him and are glad;
     they will never be disappointed.
6 The helpless call to him, and he answers;
     he saves them from all their troubles.
7 His angel guards those who fear the Lord
     and rescues them from danger.

8 Find out for yourself how good the Lord
          is!
     Happy is the man who finds safety with
          him!
9 Fear the Lord, all his people;
     those who fear him have all they need.

---

[v]Hebrew title: David pretended to be insane in the presence of
Abimelech, who sent him away; after leaving, David wrote this
psalm.

[10] Even lions lack food and go hungry,
  but those who obey the Lord lack noth-
    ing good.

[11] Come, my young friends, and listen to me,
  and I will teach you to fear the Lord.
[12] Would you like to enjoy life?
  Do you want long life and happiness?
[13] Then keep from speaking evil
  and from telling lies.
[14] Turn away from evil and do good;
  desire peace and do your best to have it.

[15] The Lord watches over the righteous
  and listens to their cries;
[16] but he opposes those who do evil,
  so that even their own people forget
    them.
[17] Righteous men call to the Lord and he
    listens;
  he rescues them from all their troubles.
[18] The Lord is near to those who are dis-
    couraged;
  he saves those who have lost all hope.

[19] The good man suffers many troubles,
  but the Lord saves him from them all;
[20] the Lord preserves him completely;
  not one of his bones is broken.
[21] Evil will kill the wicked;
  those who hate the righteous will be
    punished.

[22] The Lord will save his servants;
  those who go to him for protection will
    be spared.

A Prayer for Help

35 Oppose those who oppose me, Lord,
  and fight those who fight me!
[2] Take your shield and armour

and come to my help.
3 Lift up your spear and war axe
against those who pursue me.
Tell me that you are my Saviour!

4 May those who try to kill me
be defeated and disgraced!
May those who plot against me
be turned back and confused!
5 May they be like straw blown by the wind,
as the angel of the Lord chases them!
6 May their path be dark and slippery,
while the angel of the Lord strikes them
down!

7 Without any reason they laid a trap for me
and dug a deep hole to catch me.
8 But destruction will catch them before
they know it;
they will be caught in their own trap
and fall into the hole they dug!w

9 Then I will be glad because of the Lord;
I will be happy because he saved me.
10 With all my heart I will say to the Lord,
"There is no one like you!
You protect the weak from the strong,
the poor and needy from the oppres-
sor!"

11 Evil men testify against me
and accuse me of crimes I know nothing
about.
12 They pay me back evil for good,
and I am full of despair.
13 But when they were sick, I dressed in
mourning;
I deprived myself of food;
I prayed with my head bowed low,
14 as I would pray for a friend or a brother.

wOne ancient translation the hole they dug; Hebrew destruction.

I went around bent over in mourning,
as one who mourns for his mother.

15 When I was in trouble, they were all glad
and gathered round me to make fun of
me;
strangers beat me
and kept striking me.
16 They made me suffer, and made fun of
me*
glaring at me with hate.

17 How much longer, Lord, will you look on?
Rescue me from their attacks;
save my life from these lions!
18 Then I will thank you in the large assembly,
I will praise you before a great crowd.

19 Don't let my enemies, those liars,
gloat over my defeat!
Don't let those who hate me for no reason
wink with delight over my sorrow!

20 They do not speak in a friendly way;
instead they invent all kinds of lies
about peace-loving people.
21 They accuse me, shouting,
"We saw what you did!"
22 But you, Lord, have seen this.
So don't be silent, Lord;
don't keep yourself far away!
23 Wake up, Lord, and defend me;
rise up, my God, and plead my cause.
24 You are righteous, Lord, so declare me
innocent;
do not let my enemies gloat over me,
my God!
25 Do not let them say to themselves,
"Well! Just what we wanted!"

---

*One ancient translation they made me suffer, and made fun of me;
Hebrew with the profane of mockers of a cake.

Do not let them say,
"We have defeated him!"

26 May those who gloat over my suffering
be completely defeated and confused;
may those who claim to be better than I
am
be covered with shame and disgrace!

27 May those who are glad that I am acquit-
ted
shout with joy and say again and again,
"Great is the Lord;
he is happy with the success of his servant!"
28 Then I will proclaim your righteousness,
and I will praise you all day long.

The Wickedness of Man

36 Sin speaks to the wicked man
deep in his heart;
he rejects God, and does not fear him.
2 Because he has such a high opinion of
himself,
he thinks that God will not discover
and condemn his sin.
3 His speech is evil and full of lies;
he is no longer wise enough to do good.
4 He makes evil plans as he lies in bed;
his conduct is not good,
and he does not reject what is evil.

The Goodness of God

5 Lord, your constant love reaches the
heavens,
your faithfulness extends to the skies.
6 Your righteousness is firm like the great
mountains,

your judgements are like the depths of
the sea.
You, Lord, care for men and animals.

7 How precious, God, is your constant love!
Men find protection under the shadow
of your wings.
8 They feast on the abundant food from
your house;
you give them to drink from the river of
your goodness.
9 You are the source of all life,
and because of your light we see the
light.

10 Continue to love those who know you
and to do good to those who are righteous.
11 Do not let proud men attack me
or wicked men make me run away.
12 See where evil men have fallen!
There they lie, unable to rise.

The Destiny of the Wicked and of the Good

37 Don't be worried on account of the
wicked;
don't be jealous of those who do wrong;
2 they will disappear like grass that dries up;
they will die like plants that wither.

3 Trust in the Lord and do good;
live in the land and be safe.
4 Seek your happiness with the Lord,
and he will give you what you most
desire.

5 Give yourself to the Lord;
trust in him, and he will help you;
6 he will cause your goodness to shine as the
light
and your righteousness as the noonday
sun.

7 Be calm before the Lord, and wait patiently for him to act;
  don't be worried about those who prosper
  or those who succeed in their evil plans.

8 Don't be angry; don't get mad!
  Don't be worried! It won't do you any good.
9 Those who trust in the Lord will live safely in the land,
  but the wicked will be driven out.

10 In just a little while, the wicked will disappear;
  you may look for them, but you will not find them;
11 but those who are gentle will live safely in the land
  and enjoy complete peace.

12 The wicked man plots against the good man
  and glares at him with hate.
13 The Lord laughs at the wicked man,
  because he knows that he will soon be destroyed.

14 The wicked draw their swords and bend their bows
  to kill the poor and needy,
  to slaughter men who are good;
15 but they will be stabbed by their own swords,
  and their bows will be smashed.

16 The little that a good man owns
  is worth more than the wealth of all the wicked;
17 because the Lord will take away the strength of the wicked,
  but protect those who are good.

¹⁸ The Lord takes care of those who obey
    him,
    and the land will be theirs forever.
¹⁹ They will not suffer when times are bad;
    they will have enough in time of famine.
²⁰ But the wicked will die;
    the enemies of the Lord will vanish like
    wild flowers;
    they will disappear like smoke.

²¹ The wicked man borrows, and doesn't pay
    back,
    but the good man is generous and lib-
    eral.
²² Those who are blessed by the Lord will
    live safely in the land,
    but those who are cursed by him will be
    driven out.

²³ The Lord guides a man safely in the way
    he should go
    and is pleased with his conduct.
²⁴ If he falls, he will not stay down,
    because the Lord will help him up.

²⁵ I am old now and no longer a boy,
    but I have never seen a good man aban-
    doned by the Lord,
    or his children begging for food.
²⁶ At all times he gives freely and lends to
    others,
    and his children are a blessing.

²⁷ Turn away from evil and do good,
    and you will live in the land forever;
²⁸ because the Lord loves what is right,
    and he does not abandon his faithful
    people.
  He protects them always,
    but the descendants of the wicked will
    be driven out.

²⁹ The righteous will live safely in the land
and possess it forever.

³⁰ The good man's words are wise,
and he speaks of what is right.
³¹ He keeps the law of his God in his heart
and never departs from it.

³² The wicked man watches the good man
and tries to kill him;
³³ but the Lord will not abandon him to his
enemy's power,
or let him be condemned when he is on
trial.

³⁴ Put your hope in the Lord and obey his
commandments;
he will give you the strength to possess
the land,
and you will see the wicked driven out.

³⁵ I have seen a wicked man who was a
tyrant;
he towered over everyone like a cedar
of Lebanon;ʸ
³⁶ but later Iᶻ passed by and he wasn't there;
I looked for him, but couldn't find him.

³⁷ Notice the good man, observe the righteous man;
a peaceful man has descendants;
³⁸ but sinners are completely destroyed,
and their descendants are wiped out.

³⁹ The Lord saves righteous men
and protects them in times of trouble.
⁴⁰ He helps them and rescues them;
he saves them from the wicked,
because they go to him for protection.

ʸ One ancient translation like a cedar of Lebanon; Hebrew unclear.
ᶻ Some ancient translations I; Hebrew he.

The Prayer of a Suffering Man

38 Lord, don't be angry and rebuke me!
Don't punish me in your anger!
² You have punished me and wounded me;
you have struck me down.

³ Because of your anger, I am seriously ill;
my whole body is diseased because of
my sins.
⁴ I am drowning in the flood of my sins;
I am weighted down by their heavy
burden.

⁵ Because I have been foolish,
my sores stink and rot.
⁶ I am bent over, I am crushed;
I mourn all day long.
⁷ I am burning with fever,
and I am seriously ill.
⁸ I am utterly crushed and defeated;
my heart is troubled, and I groan with
pain.

⁹ Lord, you know what I desire;
you hear all my groans.
¹⁰ My heart is pounding, my strength is
gone,
and my eyes have lost their brightness.
¹¹ My friends and neighbours will not come
near me,
because of my sores;
even my family stays away from me.
¹² Those who want to kill me lay traps for
me,
and those who want to hurt me threaten
to ruin me;
all day long they plot against me.

¹³ I am like a deaf man, and cannot hear,
like a dumb man, and cannot speak,

¹⁴ I am like a man who does not answer,
   because he cannot hear.

¹⁵ I trust in you, Lord;
   and you, Lord my God, will answer me.
¹⁶ Don't let my enemies gloat over my dis-
   tress;
   don't let them boast about my downfall!
¹⁷ I am about to fall,
   and my pain is always with me.

¹⁸ I confess my sins,
   and they fill me with anxiety.
¹⁹ My enemies are healthy and strong;
   there are many who hate me for no
   reason.
²⁰ Those who pay back evil for good
   are against me because I try to do right.

²¹ Do not abandon me, Lord,
   do not stay away, my God!
²² Help me now, Lord my Saviour!

The Confession of a Suffering Man

39 I said, "I will be careful about
         what I do
   and not let my tongue make me sin;
I will not say anything
   while evil men are near."
² I kept quiet, not saying a word,
   not even about anything good!
But my suffering only became worse,
³   and my heart was filled with anxiety.
The more I thought, the more troubled I
      became;
   I could not keep from asking:
⁴ "Lord, how long will I live?
   When will I die?
   Teach me how soon my life may end."

⁵ How short you have made my life!
   In your sight my lifetime seems noth-
      ing.

Indeed every living man is no more than
    a puff of wind,
6   no more than a shadow!
All he does is for nothing;
    he gathers wealth, but doesn't know
    who will get it!

7 What, then, can I hope for, Lord?
    I put my hope in you.
8 Save me from all my sins
    and don't let fools make fun of me.
9 I will keep quiet, I will not say a word,
    because you made me suffer like this.
10 Don't punish me any more!
    I am about to die from your blows!
11 You punish a man's sins by your rebukes,
    and like a moth, you destroy what he
    loves.
Indeed a man is no more than a puff of
    wind!

12 Hear my prayer, Lord,
    and listen to my plea;
    don't be silent when I cry to you!
Like all my ancestors,
    I am only your guest for a little while.
13 Leave me alone so that I may have some
    happiness,
    before I go away and am no more.

A Song of Praise

40 I waited and waited for the Lord's
    help;
    then he listened to me and heard my
    cry.
2 He pulled me out of a dangerous pit,
    out of a muddy hole!
He set me safely on a rock
    and made me secure.
3 He taught me to sing a new song,

a song of praise to our God.
Many who see this will be afraid
and will put their trust in the Lord.

⁴ Happy is the person who trusts the Lord,
who does not turn to idols,
or join those who worship false gods.
⁵ You have done many things for us, Lord
my God;
there is no one like you!
You have made many wonderful plans
for us.
If I tried to speak of all of them,
there would be more than I could tell.

⁶ You do not want sacrifices and offerings;
you do not ask for animals burned
whole on the altar,
or sacrifices to take away sins.
Instead, you have given me ears to hear
you,
⁷   and so I answered, "Here I am;
your instructions for me are in the book
of the Law.
⁸ How I love to do your will, my God!
I keep your teaching in my heart."

⁹ In the meeting of all your people, Lord,
I told the good news that you save.
You know that I will never stop telling
it.
¹⁰ I have not kept the news of salvation to
myself;
I have always spoken of your faithfulness and help.
In the meeting of all your people I have
not been silent
about your constant love and loyalty.

¹¹ Lord, I know you will never stop being
merciful to me!
Your love and loyalty will always keep
me safe.

A Prayer for Help

(Psalm 70)

¹² I am surrounded by many troubles—
too many to count!
My sins have caught up with me,
and I can no longer see;
they are more than the hairs on my head,
and I have lost my courage.
¹³ Save me, Lord! Help me now!
¹⁴ May those who try to kill me
be completely defeated and confused!
May those who are happy because of my
troubles
be turned back and disgraced!
¹⁵ May those who make fun of me
be dismayed by their defeat!

¹⁶ May all who come to you
be glad and joyful!
May all who love your salvation
always say, "How great the Lord is!"

¹⁷ I am weak and helpless,
but you, Lord, think of me.
You are my helper and Saviour—
do not delay, my God!

The Prayer of a Sick Man

41 Happy is the man who is concerned
for the poor;
the Lord will help him when he is in
trouble.
² The Lord will protect him and preserve
his life;
he will make him happy in the land;
he will not abandon him to the power of
his enemies.
³ The Lord will help him when he is sick
and restore him to health.

⁴ I said, "I have sinned against you, Lord;
    be merciful to me and cure me!"
⁵ My enemies say bad things about me.
    They say, "When will he die and be for-
        gotten?"
⁶ Those who come to see me are not sin-
        cere;
    they gather all the bad news about me,
    and then go out and tell it everywhere.
⁷ All who hate me whisper to each other
        about me,
    they imagine the worst about me.
⁸ They say, "He is fatally ill
    and will never leave his bed again."
⁹ Even my best friend, the one I trusted
        most,
    the one who shared my food,
    has turned against me.

¹⁰ Be merciful to me, Lord, and restore my
        health;
    and I will pay my enemies back!
¹¹ I will know that you are pleased with me,
    because they will not triumph over me.
¹² You will help me, because I do what is
        right;
    you will keep me in your presence
        forever.

¹³ Let us praise the Lord, the God of Israel;
    praise him now and forever!
    Amen! Amen!

BOOK TWO
(Psalms 42—72)

The Prayer of a Man in Exile

42   As a deer longs for a stream of cool
            water,
    so I long for you, God.

² I thirst for you, the living God;
 when can I go and worship in your
  presence?
³ Day and night I cry,
 and tears are my only food;
all the time my enemies ask me,
 "Where is your God?"

⁴ My heart breaks when I remember the
  past,
 when I went with the crowds to the
  house of God,
and led them as they walked along,
 a happy crowd, singing and shouting
  praise to God.
⁵ Why am I so sad?
 Why am I troubled?
I will put my hope in God,
 and once again I will praise him,
 my Saviour and my God.

⁶ My heart is breaking,
 so I will remember him;
in my exile in the region of the Jordan,
 near Mount Hermon and Mount Mizar,
 I will remember him.
⁷ The ocean depths call out to each other,
 and the waterfalls of God are roaring!
They are like the waves of sorrow
 with which he floods my soul.
⁸ May the Lord show his constant love every day!
 May I sing praise to him every night,
 and pray to God, who gives me life.

⁹ To God, my defender, I say,
 "Why have you forgotten me?
Why must I go on suffering
 from the cruelty of my enemies?"
¹⁰ I am crushed by their insults,
 as they keep on asking me,
 "Where is your God?"

¹¹ Why am I so sad?
        Why am I troubled?
I will put my hope in God,
        and once again I will praise him,
        my Saviour and my God.

The Prayer of a Man in Exile
(Continuation of Psalm 42)

43   God, declare me innocent,
                and defend my cause against the
                    ungodly;
        deliver me from lying and evil men!
² You are my protector;
        why have you abandoned me?
Why must I go on suffering
        from the cruelty of my enemies?

³ Send your light and your truth;
        may they lead me
        and bring me back to Zion, your sacred
            hill,
        and to your temple, where you live!
⁴ Then I will go to your altar, God,
        because you give me joy and happiness;
I will play my harp and sing praise to you,
        God, my God!

⁵ Why am I so sad?
        Why am I troubled?
I will put my hope in God,
        and once again I will praise him,
        my Saviour and my God.

A Prayer for Protection

44   With our own ears we have heard it,
                God—
        our ancestors have told us about it,
        about the great things you did ın their
            time,

in the days of long ago:
2 how you yourself drove out the heathen,
    and established your people in their
    land;
  how you punished the other nations,
    but caused your own to prosper.
3 Your people did not conquer the land
    with their swords;
  they did not win it by their own power;
  it was by your power and your strength,
    by the assurance of your presence,
    showing that you loved them.

4 You are my king and my God;
    you give*a* victory to your people.
5 By your power we defeat our enemies;
    by your presence we overcome our ad-
    versaries.
6 I do not trust in my bow,
    or trust in my sword to save me;
7 because you have saved us from our ene-
    mies,
    you have defeated those who hate us.
8 We will always praise you
    and give thanks to you forever.

9 But now, God, you have rejected us and
    let us be defeated;
    you no longer march out with our ar-
    mies.
10 You made us run away from our enemies,
    and they took for themselves what was
    ours.
11 You allowed us to be slaughtered like
    sheep;
    you scattered us in foreign countries.
12 You sold your own people for a small
    price,
    and made no profit from the sale.

---

a Some ancient translations you give; *Hebrew* give!

¹³ Our neighbours see what you did to us,
    and they mock us and make fun of us.
¹⁴ You made us an object of contempt
    among the nations;
    they shake their heads at us in scorn.
¹⁵ I am always in disgrace,
    and I am covered with shame,
¹⁶ from hearing the sneers and insults
    of my enemies and adversaries.

¹⁷ All this has happened to us
    even though we have not forgotten you,
    or broken the covenant you made with
    us.
¹⁸ We have not been disloyal to you;
    we have not disobeyed your com-
    mands.
¹⁹ Yet you left us helpless among the wild
    animals;
    you abandoned us in deepest darkness.

²⁰ If we had stopped worshipping our God,
    and prayed to a foreign god,
²¹ you would surely have discovered it,
    because you know men's secret
    thoughts.
²² But it is for your sake that we are being
    killed all the time,
    that we are treated like sheep to be
    slaughtered.

²³ Wake up, Lord! Why are you asleep?
    Get up! Don't reject us forever!
²⁴ Why are you hiding from us?
    Don't forget our suffering and trouble!

²⁵ We fall crushed to the ground;
    we lie defeated in the dust.
²⁶ Get up and help us!
    Because of your constant love, save us!

A Royal Wedding Song

45 Beautiful words fill my mind,
as I compose this song for the king;
my tongue is like the pen of a good writer.

[2] You are the most handsome of all men;
you are an eloquent speaker;
God has always blessed you!
[3] Buckle on your sword, mighty king;
you are powerful and majestic!

[4] Ride on in majesty to victory,
for the defence of truth and justice![b]
Your strength will win you great victories!
[5] Your arrows are sharp and pierce the hearts of your enemies;
nations fall down at your feet.

[6] The throne that God has given you
will last forever and ever!
You rule over your kingdom with justice;
[7] you love what is right and hate what is evil.
That is why God, your God, has chosen you,
and has poured out more happiness on you
than on anyone else.
[8] The perfume of myrrh, aloes, and cassia is on your clothes;
musicians entertain you in ivory palaces.
[9] Among the ladies of your court are daughters of kings,
and at the right of your throne stands the queen,
wearing ornaments of finest gold.

[b]and justice; *Hebrew* and meekness of justice.

¹⁰ Bride of the king, listen to what I say—
      forget your people and your relatives.
¹¹ Your beauty will make the king desire
      you;
      he is your master, so you must obey
      him.
¹² The people of Tyre will bring you gifts;
      rich people will try to win your favour.

¹³ The princess is in the palace—how beauti-
      ful she is!
      Her gown is made of gold thread.
¹⁴ In her colourful gown she is led to the
      king,
      followed by her bridesmaids,
      and they also are brought to him.
¹⁵ With joy and gladness they come
      and enter the king's palace.

¹⁶ You, my king, will have many sons
      to take the place of your ancestors,
      and you will make them rulers over the
      whole earth.
¹⁷ My song will keep your fame alive
      forever,
      and everyone will praise you for all time
      to come.

God Is with Us

46 God is our shelter and strength,
      always ready to help in times of
      trouble.
² So we will not be afraid, even if the earth
      is shaken
      and mountains fall into the ocean
      depths;
³ even if the seas roar and rage,
      and the hills are shaken by the violence.

⁴ There is a river that brings joy to the city
      of God,
      to the sacred house of the Most High.

We will not be afraid

⁵ God lives in the city, and it will never be
    destroyed;
  at early dawn he will come to its help.
⁶ Nations are terrified, kingdoms are
    shaken;
  God roars out, and the earth dissolves.

⁷ The Lord Almighty is with us;
  the God of Jacob is our refuge!

⁸ Come, see what the Lord has done!
  See what amazing things he has done
    on earth!
⁹ He stops wars all over the world;
  he breaks bows, destroys spears,
  and sets shields on fire!
¹⁰ He says, "Stop your fighting, and know
    that I am God,
  supreme among the nations, supreme
    over the world!"

¹¹ The Lord Almighty is with us;
  the God of Jacob is our refuge!

Sing praise to God

The Supreme Ruler

47 Clap your hands for joy, all
peoples!
Praise God with loud songs!
2 The Lord, the Most High, is to be feared;
he is a great king, ruling over all the
world.
3 He gave us victory over the peoples;
he made us rule over the nations.
4 He chose for us the land where we live,
the proud possession of his people,
whom he loves.

5 God goes up to his throne!
There are shouts of joy and the blast of
trumpets,
as the Lord goes up!
6 Sing praise to God;
sing praise to our king!
God is king over all the world;
praise him with songs!

8 God sits on his sacred throne;
he rules over the nations.
9 The rulers of the nations come together

with the people^c of the God of Abraham.
The shields of all the warriors belong to
God;
he rules over all!

Zion, the City of God

48 The Lord is great, and must be
highly praised
in the city of our God, on his sacred
mountain.
2 Zion, the mountain of God, is high and
beautiful;
the city of the great king brings joy to
all the world!
3 God has shown that there is safety with
him
inside the fortresses of the city.

4 The kings gathered together
and came to attack Mount Zion.
5 When they saw it they were surprised;
they were afraid and ran away.
6 There they were seized with fear and an-
guish,
like a woman about to bear a child.

7 God destroys large ships with the east
wind.
8 We have heard about what God has done,
and now we have seen it
in the city of our God, the Lord Almighty;
he will keep the city safe forever.

9 Inside your temple, God,
we think of your constant love.
10 You are praised by people everywhere,
and your fame extends over all the
earth.

^cWith the people; *Hebrew* the people.

You rule with justice;
11   let the people of Zion be glad!
You give right judgements;
     let there be joy in the cities of Judah!

12 Walk all round Mount Zion and count its
        towers,
13   take notice of its walls, and examine its
        fortresses,
so that you may tell the next generation
14   that this God is our God, forever and
        ever;
     he will lead us for all time to come.

The Foolishness of Trusting in Riches

49   Hear this, everyone!
         Listen, all people everywhere,
2 great and small alike,
     rich and poor together.
3 I will think sensible thoughts;
     I will speak words of wisdom.
4 I will turn my attention to a riddle,
     and explain its meaning as I play the
        harp.

5 I am not afraid in times of danger,
     when I am surrounded by evil enemies,
6 by men who trust in their riches,
     who boast of their great wealth.
7 A man can never redeem himself;*d*
     he cannot pay God the price for his life,
8   because the payment for a man's life is
        too great.
What he can pay will never be enough
9   to keep him from the grave,
     to let him live forever.

10 He sees that even wise men die,
     as well as foolish and stupid men.

d Some Hebrew manuscripts himself; *other Hebrew manuscripts* his
brother.

They all leave their riches to their descendants.
11 Their graves[e] are their homes forever;
    there they stay for all time,
    even though they once had lands of
      their own.
12 A man's greatness cannot keep him from
    death;
    he will die like the animals.

13 See what happens to those who trust in
    themselves,
    the fate of those[f] who are satisfied with
      their wealth—
14 they are doomed to die like sheep,
    and death will be their shepherd.
  The righteous will triumph over them in
    the morning
    as their bodies decay in the land of the
      dead,
    far from their homes![g]
15 But God will save me;
    he will take me from the power of
      death.

16 Don't be afraid when a man becomes rich,
    when his wealth grows even greater;
17 he cannot take it with him when he dies;
    his wealth will not go to the grave with
      him.
18 Even if a man is satisfied with this life,
    and is praised because he is successful,
19 he will join all his ancestors in death,
    where the darkness lasts forever.
20 A man's greatness cannot keep him from
    death;
    he will die like the animals.

[e]Some ancient translations graves; Hebrew inner thoughts. [f]One ancient translation the fate of those; Hebrew after them. [g]Hebrew unclear.

True Worship

50 The Almighty God, the Lord,
       speaks;
   he calls to the whole earth, from east to
       west.
² God shines from Zion,
   the city perfect in its beauty.

³ Our God is coming, but not in silence;
   a raging fire is in front of him,
   a furious storm round him.
⁴ He calls heaven and earth as witnesses
   to see him judge his people.
⁵ He says, "Gather my faithful people to
       me,
   those who made a covenant with me by
       offering a sacrifice."
⁶ The heavens proclaim that God is right-
       eous,
   that he himself is judge!

⁷ "Listen, my people, and I will speak;
   I will testify against you, Israel.
   I am God, your God.
⁸ I do not reprimand you because of your
       sacrifices
   and the burnt offerings you always bring
       me.
⁹ And yet, I do not need bulls from your
       farms,
   or goats from your flocks,
¹⁰ because the animals of the woods are mine
   and the cattle on thousands of hills.
¹¹ All the wild birds are mine
   and all living things in the fields.

¹² "If I were hungry I would not tell you,
   because the world and everything in it
       is mine.
¹³ Do I eat the flesh of bulls,
   or drink the blood of goats?

The animals of the woods are mine

¹⁴ Let the giving of thanks be your sacrifice
to God,
and give the Almighty all the offerings
that you promised.
¹⁵ Call to me when trouble comes;
I will save you,
and you will praise me."

¹⁶ But God says to the wicked,
"Why should you recite my commandments?
Why should you talk about my covenant?
¹⁷ You refuse to let me correct you;
you reject my commands.
¹⁸ When you see a thief, you become his
friend,
and you associate with adulterers.

¹⁹ "You are always ready to speak evil;
you never hesitate to tell lies.
²⁰ You are ready to accuse your own brothers,
and to find fault with them.
²¹ You have done all this, and I have said
nothing,
so you thought that I am like you.
But now I will reprimand you,
and make the matter plain to you.

²² "Listen to this, you that ignore me,
or I will destroy you;
and there will be no one to save you:
²³ Giving thanks is the sacrifice that honours
me,
and I will surely save all who obey me."

A Prayer for Forgiveness[h]

51 Be merciful to me, God,
because of your constant love;

[h]Hebrew title: David wrote this psalm after the prophet Nathan had
spoken to him about his adultery with Bathsheba.

wipe away my sins,
    because of your great mercy!
2 Wash away my evil,
    and make me clean from my sin!

3 I recognise my faults;
    I am always conscious of my sins.
4 I have sinned against you—only against
      you,
    and done what you consider evil.
So you are right in judging me;
    you are justified in condemning me.
5 I have been evil from the time I was born;
    from the day of my birth I have been
      sinful.

6 A faithful heart is what you want;
    fill my mind with your wisdom.
7 Remove my sin, and I will be clean;
    wash me, and I will be whiter than
      snow.
8 Let me hear the sounds of joy and glad-
      ness;
    and though you have crushed and
      broken me,
    I will be happy once again.
9 Close your eyes to my sins,
    and wipe out all my evil.

10 Create a pure heart in me, God,
    and put a new and loyal spirit in me.
11 Do not banish me from your presence;
    do not take your holy spirit away from
      me.
12 Give me again the joy that comes from
      your salvation,
    and make my spirit obedient.
13 Then I will teach sinners your commands,
    and they will turn back to you.

14 Spare my life, God my Saviour,
    and I will gladly proclaim your right-
      eousness.

¹⁵ Help me to speak, Lord,
    and I will praise you.

¹⁶ You do not want sacrifices,
    or I would offer them;
  you are not pleased with burnt offerings.
¹⁷ My sacrifice is a submissive spirit, God;
    a submissive and obedient heart you
        will not reject.

¹⁸ God, be kind to Zion and help her;
    rebuild the walls of Jerusalem.
¹⁹ Then you will be pleased with the proper
        sacrifices,
      and with all burnt offerings;
      and bulls will be sacrificed on your altar.

God's Judgement and Grace[i]

52   Why do you boast, great man, of
          your evil?
    God's love is constant.
² You make plans to ruin others;
    your tongue is like a sharp razor.
  You are always inventing lies.
³ You love evil more than good
    and falsehood more than the truth.
⁴ You love to hurt people with your words,
      you liar!

⁵ So God will ruin you forever;
    he will take hold of you and pull you out
        of your tent;
    he will remove you from the land of the
        living.

---

[i] *Hebrew title:* David wrote this poem when Doeg, the Edomite, went
to Saul and told him that David had gone to the house of Abimelech.

⁶ Righteous people will see this and be
    afraid;
    they will laugh at you, and say,
⁷ "Look, here is a man who did not depend
        on God for safety,
    but instead trusted in his great wealth,
    and looked for security in being
        wicked!"

⁸ But I am like an olive tree growing near
        the house of God;
    I trust in his constant love forever and
        ever.
⁹ I will always thank you, God, for what
        you have done;
    in the company of your people
    I will proclaim that you are good.

The Wickedness of Men

(Psalm 14),

53 Fools say to themselves,
        "God doesn't matter."
    They are all corrupt,
        they have done terrible things;
        there is no one who does what is right.

² God looks down at men from heaven
        to see if there are any who are wise,
        any who worship him.
³ But they have all turned away,
        they are all equally bad;
    not one of them does what is right,
        not a single one.

⁴ "Don't they know?" God asks.
    "Are these evildoers ignorant?
    They live by robbing my people
        and do not pray to me."

⁵ But then they will become terrified,
    as they have never been before;
    because God scatters the bones of your
        enemies.
He will defeat them completely,
    because he has rejected them.

⁶ How I pray that salvation
    will come to Israel from Zion!
When God makes his people prosperous
        again,
    Jacob's descendants will be happy;
    the people of Israel will be glad.

A Prayer for Protection from Enemies[j]

54 Save me by your power, God;
        set me free by your might!
² Hear my prayer, God;
    listen to my words!

³ Proud men are coming to attack me;
    cruel men are trying to kill me—
    men who do not care about God.

⁴ I know that God is my helper,
    that the Lord is my defender!
⁵ May God punish my enemies with their
        own evil!
    He will destroy them because he is
        faithful.

⁶ Lord, I will gladly offer you a sacrifice;
    I will give you thanks,
    because you are good.
⁷ You have rescued me from all my
        troubles,
    and I have seen my enemies defeated.

[j]*Hebrew title:* David wrote this poem when the men of Ziph went to
Saul and told him that David was hiding in their territory.

A Prayer for Help

55 Hear my prayer, God;
don't turn away from my plea!
² Listen to me and answer me;
I am worn out by my worries.
³ I am upset by the threats of my enemies,
by oppression from the wicked.
They bring trouble on me;
they are angry with me and hate me.

⁴ Fear fills my heart,
and the terrors of death are heavy on
me.
⁵ I am gripped by fear and trembling;
I am overcome with horror.
⁶ I say, "I wish I had wings, like a dove!
I would fly away and find rest!
⁷ I would fly far away
and make my home in the desert.
⁸ I would hurry and find myself a shelter
from the raging wind and the storm."

I wish I had wings, like a dove!

⁹ Destroy them, Lord, and confuse their
speech,

because I see violence and riots in the
city.
10 Day and night they walk round the city on
its walls;
it is full of crime and trouble.
11 There is destruction everywhere;
the streets are filled with oppression
and fraud.

12 If it were an enemy making fun of me,
I could endure it;
if it were an opponent boasting over me,
I could hide myself from him.
13 But it is you, my companion,
my colleague and close friend!
14 We had intimate talks with each other,
and went with the crowd to the temple.
15 May death come suddenly upon my enemies;
may they go down alive into the land of
the dead!
Evil is in their homes and in their hearts.

16 But I call to the Lord God for help,
and he will save me.
17 My complaints and groans
go up to him morning, noon, and night,
and he will hear my voice.
18 He will bring me safely back
from the battles that I fight
against so many enemies.
19 God, who has ruled from eternity,
will hear me and defeat them;
there is nothing they can do about it,
because they do not fear him.

20 My former companion attacked his
friends;
he broke his promise.
21 His words were smoother than cream,
but there was hatred in his heart;
his words were as soothing as oil,
but they cut like sharp swords.

²² Leave your troubles with the Lord,
    and he will support you;
        he will never let a good man be de-
            feated.

²³ But you, God, will throw those murderers
        and liars into the depths below,
    before half their life is over.
As for me, I will trust in you.

A Prayer of Trust in God*k*

56 Be merciful to me, God,
        because I am being attacked;
    my enemies persecute me all the time!
² All day long my opponents attack me.
    There are so many who fight against
        me.
³ When I am afraid, O Most High,
    I put my trust in you.
⁴ I trust in God and praise his promise;
    in him I trust, and I will not be afraid.
    What can mere man do to me?

⁵ My enemies make trouble for me in ev-
        erything I do;
    they are always thinking about how to
        hurt me!
⁶ They gather in a hiding place
    and watch everything I do,
        hoping to kill me.
⁷ Punish*l* them, God, for their evil;
    defeat these people in your anger!

⁸ You know how troubled I am;
        you have kept a record of my tears.
    Aren't they listed in your book?
⁹ The day I call to you,

---

kHebrew title. This prayer was written by David after the Philistines
captured him in Gath. *lPunish; Hebrew* Save.

my enemies will be turned back.
This I know—God is on my side!
¹⁰ I trust in God and praise his promise;
I will praise the promise of the Lord.
¹¹ In him I trust, and I will not be afraid.
What can mere man do to me?

¹² God, I will offer you what I have promised;
I will give you my offering of praise,
¹³ because you have rescued me from death
and kept me from defeat.
And so I walk in the presence of God,
in the light that shines on the living.

A Prayer for Help[m]

57 Be merciful to me, God, be merciful,
because I come to you for safety.
In the shadow of your wings I find protection,
until all danger is past.
² I call to God, the Most High,
to God, who supplies all my needs.
³ He will answer from heaven and save me;
he will defeat my attackers.
God will show me his constant love and
faithfulness.

⁴ I lie down among lions,
who are ready to devour men.
Their teeth are like spears and arrows;
their tongues are like sharp swords.

⁵ God, show your greatness in the sky,
and your glory over all the earth!

⁶ My enemies have spread a net to catch
me;
I am overcome with distress.

---

[m] *Hebrew title:* David wrote this psalm after he ran away from Saul
in the cave.

They dug a pit in my path,
  but fell into it themselves.

[7] I am ready, God;
  I am completely ready!
  I will sing and praise you!
[8] Wake up, my soul!
  Wake up, my harp and lyre!
  I will wake up the sun!
[9] I will thank you among the nations, Lord!
  I will praise you among the peoples!
[10] Your constant love reaches up to heaven,
  your faithfulness to the skies.
[11] God, show your greatness in the sky,
  and your glory over all the earth!

A Prayer for God to Punish the Wicked

58 Do you really give a just decision,
     you rulers?[n]
  Do you judge all men fairly?
[2] No! You think only of the evil you will do,
  and commit crimes of violence in the
    land.

[3] Evil men go wrong all their lives;
  they tell lies from the day they are born.
[4] They are full of poison, like snakes;
  they stop up their ears, like a deaf
    cobra,
[5] which does not hear the voice of the snake
    charmer,
  or the chant of the clever magician.

[6] Break their teeth, God;
  tear out the fangs of these fierce lions,
    Lord!
[7] May they disappear like water draining
    away;

_____

[n]*Hebrew unclear.*

   may they be crushed like weeds on the
    path.*o*

8 May they be like snails that dissolve into
   slime;
   may they be like a baby born dead that
    never sees the light.

9 Before they know it, they are cut down
   like a bush;
   in his fierce anger God will blow them
    away
   while they are still living.*p*

10 The righteous will be glad when they see
   sinners punished;
   they will wade through the blood of the
    wicked.

11 Men will say, "The righteous are indeed
   rewarded;
   there is indeed a God who judges the
    world!"

A Prayer for Safety*q*

59 Save me from my enemies, my God;
    protect me from those who attack
    me!

2 Save me from those evil men;
   rescue me from those murderers!

3 Look! They are waiting to attack me;
   cruel men are gathering against me.
 It is not because of any sin or wrong I have
   done,

4 not because of any fault of mine, Lord,
   that they hurry to their places.

5 Rise, Lord God Almighty, and come to
   my help;
   see for yourself, God of Israel!

o Hebrew unclear. p Verse 9 in Hebrew is unclear. q Hebrew title: David
wrote this psalm when Saul sent men to watch his house in order to
kill him.

Wake up and punish the nations;
    show no mercy to those evil traitors!

6 They come back in the evening,
    snarling like dogs as they go about the
      city.
7 Listen to what they say!
Their tongues are like swords in their
    mouths,
    yet they ask, "Who will hear us?"

8 But you laugh at them, Lord;
    you make fun of all the nations!
9 My defender, I am protected by you;
    God, you are my refuge.
10 My God, who loves me, will come to me;
    he will let me see my enemies defeated.

11 Do not kill them, God, so that my people
    will not forget.
    Scatter them by your strength and de-
      stroy them,
    Lord, our protector!
12 Sin is on their lips; all their words are
    sinful;
    may they be caught in their pride!
Because they curse and lie,
13   destroy them in your anger;
    destroy them completely.
Then all people will know that God rules
    in Israel,
    that his rule extends over all the earth!

14 My enemies come back in the evening,
    snarling like dogs as they go about the
      city.
15 They roam around looking for food
    and complain if they do not get enough.

16 But I will sing about your strength;
    every morning I will sing aloud of your
      constant love.

You have been a refuge for me,
　　a shelter in my days of trouble.
¹⁷ I will praise you, my defender;
　　my refuge is God,
　　the God who loves me.

A Prayer for Deliverance[r]

60 You have rejected us, God, and defeated us;
　　you have been angry with us—but now
　　　turn back to us!
² You have made the land tremble, and you
　　have cut it open;
　　now heal its wounds because it is about
　　　to fall apart!
³ You have made your people suffer much
　　trouble;
　　you have given us wine that made us
　　　drunk.
⁴ You raised a banner for those who fear
　　you,
　　but they turned and ran from the
　　　enemy.
⁵ Save us by your might; answer our prayer,
　　so that the people you love may be
　　　rescued.

⁶ In his sanctuary God has said,
　　"In triumph I will divide Shechem,
　　and distribute Succoth Valley to my
　　　people.
⁷ Gilead is mine, and Manasseh too;
　　Ephraim is my helmet,
　　and Judah my royal sceptre.
⁸ But I will use Moab as my washbowl
　　and Edom as my sandal box.
　　Did Philistia think she would shout in
　　　triumph over me?"

[r]Hebrew title: A psalm of David, for teaching, written when he was
fighting against the Arameans from Naharaim and from Zobah, and
Joab turned back and killed 12,000 Edomites in the Salt Valley.

⁹ Who will take me, God, into the fortified
    city?
  Who will bring me to Edom?
¹⁰ Have you really rejected us?
   Aren't you going to march out with our
     armies?
¹¹ Help us fight the enemy,
   because human help is worthless!
¹² With God on our side we will win;
   he will defeat our enemies.

Take me to a safe refuge

A Prayer for Protection

61 Hear my cry, God;
        listen to my prayer!
² In my despair, far from home,
  I call to you!

  Take me to a safe refuge,
³   because you are my protector,
    my strong defender against my ene-
      mies.

⁴ Let me live in your tent all my life;
    let me find safety under your wings.
⁵ You have heard my promises, God,
    and you have given me what belongs to
       those who honour you.

⁶ Add many years to the king's life;
    let him live on and on!
⁷ May he rule forever in your presence,
       God;
    protect him with your constant love
       and faithfulness.

⁸ So I will always sing praises to you,
    as I offer you daily what I have prom-
       ised.

Confidence in God's Protection

62 I depend on God alone;
    my salvation comes from him.
² He alone is my protector and Saviour;
    he is my defender,
    and I shall never be defeated.

³ How much longer will all of you attack a
       man to defeat him,
    like a falling wall,
    like a broken-down fence?
⁴ You only want to bring him down from his
       place of honour;
    you take pleasure in lies.
You speak words of blessing,
    but in your heart you curse him.

⁵ I depend on God alone;
    I put my hope in him.
⁶ He alone is my protector and Saviour;
    he is my defender,
    and I shall never be defeated.
⁷ My salvation and honour depend on God;
    he is my strong protector;
    he is my shelter.

⁸ My people, trust in God at all times!
  Tell him all your troubles,
    because he is our refuge

⁹ Men are like a puff of breath;
  mortal men are worthless.
  Put them on the scales and they weigh
    nothing;
    they are lighter than a mere breath.
¹⁰ Don't put your trust in violence;
  don't hope to gain anything by robbery;
  even if your riches increase,
    don't depend on them.

¹¹ More than once I have heard God say
  that power belongs to him,
¹²   and that his love is constant.

  You yourself, Lord, reward every man
    according to his deeds.

Longing for God^s

63 God, you are my God,
      and I long for you.
  My whole being desires you;
    my soul is thirsty for you,
      like a dry, worn-out, and waterless land.
² Let me see you in the sanctuary;
    let me see how mighty and glorious you
      are.
³ Your constant love is better than life
      itself,
    and so I will praise you.
⁴ I will give thanks to you as long as I live;
    I will raise my hands to you in prayer.
⁵ My soul will feast, and be satisfied
    and I will sing glad songs of praise to
      you.

^s*Hebrew title:* David wrote this psalm when he was in the desert of
Judea.

⁶ As I lie in bed I remember you;
　　all night long I think of you,
⁷ because you have always been my help.
　　In the shadow of your wings I sing for
　　　　joy.
⁸ I cling to you,
　　and your hand keeps me safe.

⁹ Those who are trying to kill me
　　will go down into the land of the dead;
¹⁰ they will be killed in battle,
　　and their bodies eaten by wolves.
¹¹ The king will rejoice because of God;
　　all who make promises in God's name
　　　　will be glad,
　　but the mouths of liars will be shut.

A Prayer for Protection

64 I am in trouble, God—listen to my
　　　　prayer!
　　I am afraid—save me from my enemies!
² Protect me from the plots of the wicked,
　　from mobs of evil men.
³ They sharpen their tongues like swords,
　　and aim cruel words like arrows.
⁴ From ambush they shoot their arrows at
　　　　good men;
　　they shoot suddenly, and are not afraid.
⁵ They encourage each other in their evil
　　　　plots;
　　they talk about where they will place
　　　　their traps.
　　"No one must see them," they say.
⁶ They make evil plans, and say,
　　"We have planned a perfect crime."
　　The heart and mind of man are a mystery!

⁷ But God shoots his arrows at them,
　　and suddenly they are wounded.

8 He will destroy them because of their
     words;[t]
  all who see them will shake their heads.
9 They will all be afraid;
     they will tell what God has done
     and think about his acts.
10 All righteous people will rejoice because
     of what the Lord has done;
     they will find safety in him;
     all good people will praise him.

Praise and Thanksgiving

65 God, people must praise you in Zion
     and give you what they have
     promised,
2   because you answer prayers.
  All men shall come to you
3   on account of their sins.
  Our faults defeat us,[u]
     but you forgive them.
4 Happy are those whom you choose,
     whom you bring to live in your sanctu-
     ary!
  We shall be satisfied with the good things
     of your house,
     the blessings of your sacred temple!

5 You answer us, God our Saviour,
     and you save us by doing wonderful
     things.
  People all over the world,
     and across the distant seas, trust in you.
6 You set the mountains in place by your
     strength,
     showing your mighty power.
7 You calm the roar of the seas
     and the noise of the waves;

[t] He will destroy them because of their words; *Hebrew* They will destroy him, their words are against them. [u] *One ancient transla-tion* us; *Hebrew* me.

you calm the uproar of the peoples.
⁸ The whole world is afraid,
  because of the great things that you
    have done.
Your actions bring shouts of joy
  from one end of the earth to the other.

⁹ You show your care for the land by send-
    ing rain;
  you make it rich and fertile.
The streams you have given never run
    dry;
    they provide the earth with crops—
    this is what you have done.
¹⁰ You send abundant rain on the ploughed
    fields
    and soak them with water;
  you soften the soil with showers
    and cause the young plants to grow.
¹¹ What a rich harvest your goodness pro-
    vides!
  Wherever you go there is plenty!
¹² The pastures are filled with flocks;
  the hillsides are full of joy.
¹³ The fields are covered with sheep;
  the valleys are full of wheat;
  they shout and sing for joy!

A Song of Praise and Thanksgiving

66 Praise God with shouts of joy, all
          people!
² Sing to the glory of his name;
  offer him glorious praise!
³ Say to God, "How wonderful are the
    things you do!
  Your power is so great
  that your enemies bow in fear before
    you.
⁴ Everyone on earth worships you;
  they sing praises to you,
  they sing praises to your name."

Sing to the glory of his name

⁵ Come and see what God has done,
  his wonderful acts among men.
⁶ He changed the sea into dry land;
  our ancestors crossed the river on foot.
There we rejoiced because of what he had
  done.
⁷ He rules forever by his might
  and keeps his eyes on the nations.
  Let no rebels rise against him!

⁸ Praise our God, all nations;
  let your praise be heard.
⁹ He has kept us alive
  and has not allowed us to fall.
¹⁰ You have put us to the test, God;
  as silver is purified by fire,
  so you have tested us.
¹¹ You let us fall into a trap
  and placed heavy burdens on our backs.
¹² You let our enemies trample us;
  we went through fire and flood,
  but now you have brought us to a place
  of safety.ʸ

¹³ I will bring burnt offerings to your house;
  I will offer you what I promised.

ʸ*Some ancient translations* safety; *Hebrew* overflowing.

14 I will give you what I said I would,
       when I was in trouble.
15 I will offer sheep to be burned on the altar;
       there will be the aroma of burning
           goats;
       I will sacrifice bulls and goats.

16 Come and listen, all who honour God,
       and I will tell you what he has done for
           me.
17 I cried to him for help;
       I was ready to praise him with songs.
18 If I had ignored my sins,
       the Lord would not have listened to me.
19 But God has indeed heard me;
       he has listened to my prayer.

20 I praise God,
       because he did not reject my prayer,
       or keep back his constant love from me.

A Song of Thanksgiving

67 God, be merciful to us and bless us;
       look on us with kindness,
2 that the whole world may know your will;
       that all nations may know your salva-
           tion.

3 May the peoples praise you, God;
       may all peoples praise you!

4 May the nations be glad and sing for joy,
       because you judge the peoples with jus-
           tice
       and guide all the nations.

5 May the peoples praise you, God;
       may all peoples praise you!

6 The land has produced its harvest;

God, our God, has blessed us.
⁷ God has blessed us;
　　may all people everywhere honour him.

A National Song of Triumph

68　May God rise up and scatter his
　　　　enemies!
　　May those who hate him run away from
　　　　him!
² As smoke is blown away, so he will drive
　　them off;
　　as wax melts in front of the fire,
　　so will the wicked perish in God's pres-
　　　　ence.
³ But the righteous will be glad and rejoice
　　in his presence;
　　they will be exceedingly happy.

⁴ Sing to God, sing praise to his name;
　　prepare a way for him who rides on the
　　　　clouds.
　　His name is the Lord—be glad in his
　　　　presence!

⁵ God, who lives in his sacred temple,
　　cares for orphans and protects widows.
⁶ He gives the lonely a home to live in
　　and leads prisoners out into happy free-
　　　　dom;
　　but rebels will live in a desolate land.

⁷ God, when you led your people,
　　when you marched across the desert,
⁸ the earth shook, and the sky poured down
　　rain,
　　because of the coming of the God of
　　　　Sinai,
　　the coming of the God of Israel.
⁹ You caused abundant rain to fall,
　　and restored your worn-out land;
¹⁰ your people made their home there;

in your goodness you provided for the
poor.

11 The Lord gave the command,
and many women carried the news:
12 "Kings and their armies are running
away!"
The women at home divided what was
captured;
13   they looked like doves covered with
silver,
whose wings glitter with fine gold.
(Why did some of you stay in the sheep
pens?)
14 When Almighty God scattered the kings
on Mount Zalmon,
he caused snow to fall there.

15 What a mighty mountain is Bashan,
a mountain of many peaks!
16 Why do you, from your mighty peaks,
look with scorn
on the mountain that God chose to live
on?
The Lord will live there forever!

17 With his many thousands of mighty chariots,
the Lord comes from Sinai*w* into the
holy place.
18 He goes up to the heights,
taking many captives with him;
he receives gifts from rebellious men.
The Lord God will live there.

19 Praise the Lord,
who carries our burdens day after day;
he is the God who saves us.
20 Our God is a God who saves;
he is the Lord, our Lord,
who rescues us from death.

*w*comes from Sinai; *Hebrew* in them, Sinai.

²¹ God will surely break the heads of his
enemies,
of those who persist in their sinful ways.
²² The Lord has said, "I will bring your
enemies back from Bashan;
I will bring them back from the depths
of the ocean,
²³ that you may wade^x in their blood,
and your dogs may lap up as much as
they want."

²⁴ God, your march of triumph is seen by all,
the procession of God, my king, into his
sanctuary.
²⁵ The singers are in front, the musicians are
behind,
in between are the girls beating the tam-
bourines.
²⁶ "Praise God in the meeting of his people;
praise the Lord, all the descendants of
Israel!"
²⁷ First comes Benjamin, the smallest tribe,
then the leaders of Judah with their
group,
followed by the leaders of Zebulun and
Naphtali.

²⁸ Show your power, God,
the power you have used on our behalf.
²⁹ From your temple in Jerusalem,
where kings bring gifts to you,
³⁰ reprimand Egypt, that wild animal in the
reeds;
reprimand the nations, that herd of
bulls with their calves,
until they all bow down and offer you
their silver.^y
Scatter those people who love to make
war!

---

^x*Some ancient translations* wade; *Hebrew* break. ^y*The Hebrew text is
unclear.*

³¹ Ambassadors[z] will come from Egypt;
    the Ethiopians will raise their hands in
      prayer to God.

³² Sing to God, kingdoms of the world,
    sing praise to the Lord,
³³ to him who rides in the sky,
    the ancient sky!
Listen to him shout with a mighty roar!
³⁴ Proclaim God's power;
    his majesty is over Israel,
    his might is in the skies.
³⁵ How wonderful is God in[a] his sanctuary,
    the God of Israel!
He gives strength and power to his people.

Praise God!

A Cry for Help

69 Save me, God!
    The water is up to my neck;
² I am sinking in deep mud,
    and there is no solid ground;
I am out in deep water,
    and the waves are about to drown me.
³ I am worn out from calling for help,
    and my throat is aching;
my eyes are strained
    from looking for your help.

⁴ Those who hate me for no reason
    are more numerous than the hairs on
      my head;
those who lie about why they are my
      enemies
    are strong and want to kill me.
They made me give up things I did not
    steal.

---

[z]*Some ancient translations* Ambassadors; *Hebrew unclear.* [a]*One ancient translation* in; *Hebrew* from.

⁵ My sins, God, are not hidden from you;
   you know how foolish I have been!
⁶ Don't let me bring shame to those who
      trust in you,
      Lord God Almighty!
   Don't let me bring disgrace to those who
      worship you,
      God of Israel!
⁷ It is for your sake that I have been in-
      sulted,
   and that I am covered with shame.
⁸ I am like a stranger to my brothers,
   like a foreigner to my family.

⁹ My devotion for your temple burns in me
      like a fire;
   the insults which are hurled at you fall
      on me.
¹⁰ I humble myself[b] by fasting,
   and people insult me;
¹¹ I dress myself in clothes of mourning,
   and they make fun of me.
¹² They talk about me in the streets,
   and drunkards make songs about me.

¹³ But as for me, I will pray to you, Lord;
   answer me, God, at a time you choose,
   because of your great love,
   because you keep your promise to save.
¹⁴ Save me from sinking in the mud;
   keep me safe from my enemies,
   and from the deep water.
¹⁵ Don't let the flood come over me;
   don't let me drown in the depths,
   or sink into the grave.

¹⁶ Answer me, Lord, in the goodness of your
      constant love;
   in your great compassion, turn to me!
¹⁷ Don't hide yourself from your servant;
   I am in great trouble—answer me now!

---

b Some ancient translations humble myself; *Hebrew* cry.

¹⁸ Come to me and save me;
   rescue me from my enemies.

¹⁹ You know how I am insulted,
   how I am disgraced and dishonoured;
   you see all my enemies.
²⁰ Insults have broken my heart,
   and I am helpless.
   I had hoped for sympathy, but there was
      none;
   for comfort, but I found none.
²¹ When I was hungry, they gave me poison;
   when I was thirsty, they offered me
      vinegar.

²² May their feasts cause their ruin;
   may their celebrations*c* cause their
      downfall!
²³ Blind them so they cannot see;
   make their backs always weak!
²⁴ Pour out your anger on them;
   let your indignation overtake them!
²⁵ May their camps be left deserted;
   may no one be left alive in their tents!
²⁶ They persecute those whom you have
      punished;
   they talk about the sufferings of those
      you have wounded.
²⁷ Keep a record of all their sins;
   don't let them have any part in your
      salvation.
²⁸ May their names be erased from the book
      of the living;
   may they not be included in the list of
      your people.

²⁹ But I am needy and in pain;
   lift me up, God, and save me!

³⁰ I will praise God with a song;

---

cOne ancient translation their celebrations; *Hebrew* those who are at peace.

I will proclaim his greatness by giving
    him thanks.
³¹ This will please the Lord more than offer-
      ing him an ox,
    more than giving him a full-grown bull.
³² When the needy see this they will be glad;
    those who worship God will be en-
      couraged.
³³ The Lord listens to those in need,
    and does not forget his people in prison.

³⁴ Praise God, heaven and earth,
    the seas and all creatures in them!
³⁵ He will save Zion,
    and rebuild the towns of Judah;
his people will live there and possess the
    land;
³⁶   the descendants of his servants will in-
      herit it,
    and those who love him will live there.

A Prayer for Help

(Psalm 40.13-17)

70 Save me, God!
    Lord, help me now!
² May those who try to kill me
    be defeated and confused!
May those who are happy because of my
    troubles
    be turned back and disgraced!
³ May those who make fun of me
    be dismayed by their defeat!

⁴ May all who come to you
    be glad and joyful!
May all who love your salvation
    always say, "How great God is!"

⁵ I am weak and helpless;
    come quickly to me, God.

You are my helper and Saviour—
    do not delay, Lord!

An Old Man's Prayer

71 Lord, I am safe with you;
        never let me be defeated!
2 Because you are righteous, help me and
        rescue me.
    Listen to me and save me!
3 Be my secure shelter,
    and a strong fortress[d] to protect me;
    you are my refuge and defence.

4 My God, rescue me from wicked men,
    from the power of cruel and evil men.
5 Lord, I put my hope in you;
    I have trusted in you since I was young.
6 I have relied on you all my life;
    you have protected[e] me since I was
        born;
    I will always praise you!

7 My life has been a mystery to many,
    but you are my strong defender.
8 All day long I praise you
    and proclaim your glory.
9 Do not reject me now that I am old;
    do not abandon me now that I am fee-
        ble!
10 My enemies want to kill me;
    they talk and plot against me.
11 They say, "God has abandoned him;
    let us go after him and catch him,
    because there is no one to rescue him!"

12 Don't stay so far away, God;
    my God, help me now!
13 May those who attack me
    be defeated and destroyed!

---

[d]One ancient translation a strong fortress; Hebrew to go always you
commanded. [e]Some ancient translations protected; Hebrew unclear.

I am old and my hair is grey

May those who try to hurt me
   be shamed and disgraced!
¹⁴ I will always put my hope in you;
   I will praise you more and more.
¹⁵ I will tell of your righteousness;
   all day long I will speak of your salva-
      tion,
   though it is more than I can understand.
¹⁶ I will praise your power, Lord God;
   I will proclaim your righteousness,
      yours alone.

¹⁷ You have taught me ever since I was
      young,

and I still tell of your wonderful acts.
¹⁸ Now that I am old and my hair is grey,
    do not abandon me, God!
  Be with me while I proclaim your power
    and might
      to all generations to come.

¹⁹ Your righteousness, God, reaches the
    skies.
  You have done great things;
  there is no one like you!
²⁰ You have sent troubles and suffering on
    me,
  but you will restore my strength;
  you will keep me from the grave.
²¹ You will make me greater than ever;
  you will comfort me again.

²² I will indeed praise you with the harp;
  I will praise your faithfulness, my God.
  On my harp I will play hymns to you,
    the Holy One of Israel.
²³ I will shout for joy as I play for you;
  with my whole being I will sing,
  because you have saved me.
²⁴ I will speak of your righteousness all day
    long,
  because those who tried to harm me
  have been defeated and disgraced.

A Prayer for the King

72 Teach the king to judge with your
    righteousness, God,
  share with him your own justice,
² so that he will rule over your people with
    justice,
  and govern the poor with righteousness.
³ May the land enjoy prosperity;
  may it experience righteousness.
⁴ May the king judge the poor fairly;
  may he help the needy

and defeat the oppressors!
5 May your people worship you as long as
the sun shines,
    as long as the moon gives light, for all
    time.

6 May the king be like rain on the fields,
    like showers falling on the land.
7 May righteousness flourish in his lifetime,
    and prosperity last as long as the moon
    shines.

8 His kingdom will reach from sea to sea,
    from the Euphrates River to the ends of
    the earth.
9 The peoples of the desert will bow down
    before him;
    his enemies will lie flat in the dust.
10 The kings of Spain and of the islands will
    offer him gifts;
    the kings of Arabia and Ethiopia will
    bring him offerings.
11 All the kings will bow down before him;
    all nations will serve him!

12 He rescues the poor who call to him,
    and those who are needy and neglected.
13 He has pity on the weak and poor;
    he saves the lives of those in need.
14 He rescues them from oppression and vio-
    lence;
    their lives are precious to him.

15 Long live the king!
    May he be given gold from Arabia;
    may prayers be said for him at all times;
    may God's blessings be on him always!
16 May there be plenty of grain in the land;
    may the hills be covered with crops,
    as fruitful as those of Lebanon.
    May the cities be filled with people,
    like grass growing in the fields.

¹⁷ May his name never be forgotten;
    may his fame last as long as the sun.
May all nations praise him,
    may all people ask God to bless them
    as he has blessed the king.

¹⁸ Praise the Lord, the God of Israel,
    who alone does these wonderful things!
¹⁹ Praise his glorious name forever,
    and may his glory fill the whole earth!
    Amen! Amen!

²⁰ The end of the prayers of David, the son
    of Jesse.

BOOK THREE
(Psalms 73–89)

The Justice of God

73 God is indeed good to Israel,
    to those who have pure hearts!
² But I was about to fall down;
    my feet were about to slip,
³ because I was jealous of the proud,
    and I saw that the wicked are rich.

⁴ They do not suffer pain;
    they are strong and healthy.
⁵ They don't suffer as other men do;
    they don't have the troubles that others
      have.
⁶ And so they wear pride like a necklace,
    and violence like a robe;
⁷ their hearts pour out evil,ᶠ
    and their minds are filled with wicked
      schemes.
⁸ They make fun of others and speak of evil
      things;

ᶠSome ancient translations their hearts pour out evil; Hebrew unclear.

they are proud and talk about oppress-
ing others.

9 They speak evil of God in heaven,
and give arrogant orders to men on
earth,

10 so that even God's people turn to them
and eagerly believe all they say.g

11 They say, "God will not know;
the Most High will not find out!"

12 This is what the wicked are like.
They have plenty and are always getting more.

13 Is it for nothing, then, that I have kept
myself pure,
and my hands clean from sin?

14 God, you have made me suffer all day
long;
every morning you have punished me!

15 If I had said such things,
I would have been untrue to your people.

16 So I tried hard to understand this,
even though it was so difficult,

17 until I went into your temple
and understood what will happen to the
wicked.

18 Surely you put them in slippery places
and make them fall to destruction!

19 They are instantly destroyed;
they go down to a horrible end!

20 Lord, they are like a dream that goes away
in the morning;
when you wake up you forget what they
were like.

21 When my thoughts were bitter,
and my feelings were hurt,

22 I was stupid, and did not understand;
I acted like an animal towards you.

gHebrew unclear.

²³ Yet I am always with you,
and you hold me by the hand.
²⁴ You guide me with your advice,
and at the end you will receive me with
honour.
²⁵ What else do I have in heaven but you?
since I have you, what else do I want on
earth?
²⁶ My mind and my body may grow weak,
but God is my strength;
he is all I ever want!

²⁷ Surely those who abandon you will die,
and you will destroy those who are unfaithful to you.
²⁸ But as for me, how wonderful to be near
God!
In the Lord God I find protection,
to proclaim all that he has done.

A Prayer for National Deliverance

74 Why have you abandoned us like
this, God?
Will you be angry with your own people
forever?
² Remember your people, whom you chose
to be yours a long time ago,
the people you redeemed to be your
own tribe.
Remember Mount Zion, where you
have lived!
³ Come and walk over these total ruins;
our enemies have destroyed everything
in the temple!

⁴ Your enemies shout in triumph in your
meeting place;
they have taken over the temple.
⁵ They looked like woodsmen
cutting down trees with their axes.
⁶ They smashed all the wooden panels

with their axes and battering rams.
⁷ They set your temple on fire;
    they profaned the place where you are
        worshipped;
    they wrecked it all.
⁸ They decided to crush us completely;
    they burned down every holy place in
        the land.

⁹ All our sacred symbols are gone;
    there are no prophets left,
    and no one knows how long this will
        last.
¹⁰ How long, God, will our enemies make
        fun of us?
    Will they insult your name forever?
¹¹ Why have you refused to help us?
    Why do you keep your hands behind
        you?ʰ

¹² But God, you have been our king from the
        beginning;
    you win victories on earth.
¹³ With your mighty strength you divided
        the sea
    and smashed the heads of the sea mon-
        sters;
¹⁴ you crushed the heads of the monster
        Leviathan,
    and gave the desert people his dead
        body to eat.
¹⁵ You made springs and fountains flow;
    you dried up large rivers.
¹⁶ You created the day and the night;
    you set the sun and the moon in their
        places;
¹⁷ you set the limits of the earth;
    you made summer and winter.

¹⁸ But remember, Lord, that your enemies
        make fun of you;

ʰWhy do you keep your hands behind you; *Hebrew unclear.*

that they are foolish and despise you.
[19] Don't abandon your helpless people to
    their cruel enemies;
    don't forget your persecuted people!

[20] Remember the covenant you made with
    us.
    There is violence in every dark corner
    of the land!
[21] Don't let the oppressed be defeated,
    but let the poor and needy praise you.

[22] Rise, God, and defend your cause!
    Remember that the godless make fun of
    you all day long!
[23] Don't forget the angry shouts of your ene-
    mies,
    the continuous noise made by your
    foes.

God the Judge

75 We praise you, God, we praise you!
    We proclaim how great you are,
and tell the wonderful things you have
    done!

[2] "I have set a time for judgement," says
    God,
    "and I will judge with fairness.
[3] Though the earth and all who live on it
    disappear,
    I will keep its foundations firm.
[4] I tell the proud not to brag,
    and the wicked not to be arrogant;
[5] I tell them to quit showing off,
    and to stop their bragging."

[6] Judgement does not come from the east or
    from the west,

[i]Some ancient translations We proclaim how great you are, and tell;
Hebrew Your name is near and they tell.

from the north or from the south;
⁷ it is God who does the judging,
    putting some down and lifting others
      up.
⁸ The Lord holds a cup in his hand,
    full of fresh wine, very strong;
  he pours it out, and all the wicked drink
      it;
    they drink it down to the last drop.

⁹ But I will never stop speaking of the God
    of Jacob,
    or singing praises to him.
¹⁰ He will break the power of the wicked,
    but the power of the righteous will be
     increased.

God the Victor

76 God is well known in Judah,
    and famous in Israel.
² He has his home in Jerusalem;
    he lives on Mount Zion.
³ There he broke the arrows of the enemies,
    their shields and swords, yes, all their
     weapons.

⁴ How glorious you are, God!
    How majestic, as you return from the
     mountains
    where you defeated your foes!
⁵ Their brave soldiers have been stripped of
    their loot,
    and are now sleeping the sleep of death;
    there is no one left to use their weapons.
⁶ When you threatened them, God of
    Jacob,
    the horses and their riders fell dead.

⁷ But you—how men fear you!

^jfrom the north or from the south; *Hebrew* from the mountains of the
south.

Who can stand in your presence
when you are angry?
[8] You made your judgement known from
heaven;
the earth was afraid and lay still,
[9] when you rose up to pronounce judgement,
to save all the oppressed on earth.

[10] Men's anger only results in more praise
for you;
those who survive the wars will keep
your festivals.[k]
[11] Give the Lord your God what you promised him;
all you nearby nations bring gifts to
him.
God makes men fear him;
[12]   he humiliates proud princes,
and terrorizes great kings.

Comfort in Time of Distress

77 I cry aloud to God;
I cry aloud, and he hears me.
[2] In time of trouble I pray to the Lord;
all night long I lift my hands in prayer,
but I cannot find comfort.
[3] I think of God, and I sigh;
I meditate, and I feel discouraged.

[4] He doesn't let me sleep;
I am so worried that I cannot speak.
[5] I think of days gone by
and remember years of long ago.
[6] I spend the night in deep thought;[l]
I meditate, and this is what I ask myself:

[7] "Will the Lord always reject me?
Will he never again be pleased with me?

[k]*One ancient translation* will keep your festivals; *Hebrew unclear.*
[l]*Some ancient translations* deep thought; *Hebrew song.*

8 Has he stopped loving me?
   Is his promise no longer good?
9 Has God forgot to be merciful?
   Has anger taken the place of his com-
      passion?"
10 Then I said, "What hurts me most is
      this—
   that God is no longer powerful."

11 I will remember your great acts, Lord;
   I will recall the wonders you did in the
      past.
12 I will think about all that you have done;
   I will meditate on all your deeds.

13 Everything you do, God, is holy!
   No god is as great as you!
14 You are the God who works miracles;
   you showed your might among the na-
      tions.
15 By your power you saved your people,
   the descendants of Jacob and of Joseph.

16 When the waters saw you, God, they were
      afraid,
   and the depths of the sea trembled.
17 The clouds poured down rain;
   thunder crashed from the sky,
   and lightning flashed in all directions.
18 The crash of your thunder rolled out,
   and flashes of lightning lit up the whole
      world;
   the earth trembled and shook.
19 You walked through the sea;
   you crossed the deep ocean,
   but your footprints could not be seen.
20 You led your people like a shepherd,
   with Moses and Aaron in charge of
      them.

God and His People

78 Listen, my people, to my teaching,
and pay attention to what I say.
2 I am going to speak to you,
and tell you mysteries from the past,
3 things we have heard and known,
that our ancestors have told us.
4 We will not keep them from our children,
but will tell the next generation
about the Lord's power and his mighty
acts,
and the wonderful things that he has
done.

5 He gave laws to the people of Israel,
and commandments to the descendants
of Jacob.
He gave orders to our ancestors
to teach his laws to their children,
6 so that the next generation might learn
them,
and in turn should tell their children.
7 In this way they also would put their trust
in God,
and not forget what he had done,
but always obey his commandments.
8 They should not be like their ancestors,
a rebellious and disobedient people,
whose trust in God was never firm,
and who did not remain faithful to him.

9 The Ephraimites, who fought with bows
and arrows,
ran away on the day of battle.
10 They did not keep their covenant with
God;
they refused to obey his law.
11 They forgot what he had done,
the miracles that he had shown them.
12 While their ancestors watched, God performed a miracle

in the field of Zoan, in the land of
Egypt.
¹³ He divided the sea and led them through;
he made the waters stand like walls.
¹⁴ By day he led them with a cloud,
and all night long with the light of a fire.
¹⁵ He split rocks open in the desert,
and gave them water from the depths.
¹⁶ He caused a stream to come out of the
rock,
and made the water flow like a river.

¹⁷ But they continued to sin against God,
and rebelled in the desert against the
Most High.
¹⁸ They deliberately put God to the test,
by demanding the food they wanted.
¹⁹ They spoke against God, saying,
"Can God set a table in the desert?
²⁰ It is true that he struck the rock,
and water flowed out in a torrent;
but can he also provide us with bread,
and give his people meat?"

²¹ And so the Lord was angry when he heard
them;
he attacked his people with fire,
and his anger against them grew,
²² because they had no faith in him,
and didn't believe that he would save
them.
²³ But he spoke to the sky above,
and commanded its doors to open:
²⁴ he gave them grain from heaven,
by sending down manna for them to
eat.
²⁵ So they ate the food of angels.
God gave them all they could eat.
²⁶ Then he caused the east wind to blow,
and by his power he stirred up the south
wind,
²⁷ and sent down birds on them as thick as
dust,

as many as the grains of sand on the
   shore;
²⁸ they fell in the middle of the camp,
      all round the tents.
²⁹ So the people ate and were satisfied;
      God gave them all they wanted.
³⁰ But while they were still eating,
      even before they had satisfied them-
         selves,
³¹ God became angry with them,
      and killed the strongest men,
      the best young men of Israel!

³² In spite of all his miracles the people kept
      on sinning,
      and would not believe;
³³ so he ended their days like a breath,
      their lives with sudden disaster.
³⁴ But when he would kill some of them,
      the rest would turn to him;
      they would repent and pray earnestly to
         him.
³⁵ They remembered that God was their
      protector,
      that the Most High was their Saviour.
³⁶ But their words were all lies,
      and everything they said was flattery.
³⁷ They were not loyal to him;
      they were not faithful to their covenant
         with him.

³⁸ But God was merciful to his people.
      He forgave their sin
      and did not destroy them.
   Many times he kept from being angry
      and restrained his fury.
³⁹ He remembered that they were only men,
      and like a wind that blows by and is
         gone.

⁴⁰ How often they rebelled against him in
      the desert;

how many times they made him sad!
41 Again and again they put God to the test,
   and made the Holy One of Israel angry.
42 They forgot his great power;
   they forgot the time he saved them
      from their enemies,
43 and performed his mighty acts and mira-
      cles
   in the field of Zoan, in the land of
      Egypt.
44 He turned the rivers into blood,
   so that the Egyptians couldn't drink
      from their streams.
45 He sent flies among them, that tormented
      them,
   and frogs, that ruined their fields.
46 He sent caterpillars to eat their crops,
   and grasshoppers to destroy their fields.
47 He killed their grapevines with hail,
   and their fig trees with frost.
48 He killed their cattle with hail,
   and their flocks with lightning.
49 He blasted them with his furious anger
      and fierce rage;
   he caused them great distress
   by sending the destroying angels.
50 He did not restrain his anger,
   or spare their lives,
   but killed them with a plague.
51 He killed the firstborn sons
   of all the families in Egypt.

52 Then he led his people out like a shep-
      herd;
   he guided them through the desert.
53 He led them safely, and they were not
      afraid;
   but the sea covered their enemies.
54 He brought them to his holy land,
   to the mountains which he himself con-
      quered.
55 He drove out the inhabitants as his people
      advanced;

he divided the land among the tribes of
  Israel,
and there let them settle in their tents.

⁵⁶ But they rebelled against Almighty God,
    and put him to the test.
  They did not obey his commandments,
⁵⁷   but were rebellious and disloyal like
      their ancestors,
      unreliable as arrows shot from a
        crooked bow.
⁵⁸ They angered him with their heathen
    places of worship,
    and made him jealous with their idols.
⁵⁹ God was angry when he saw it,
    and so rejected his people completely.
⁶⁰ He abandoned his tent in Shiloh,
    the home where he had lived among
      men.
⁶¹ He allowed the enemies to capture the
    covenant box,
    where his power and glory were seen.
⁶² He was angry with his own people,
    and let them be killed by their enemies.
⁶³ Young men were killed in war,
    and young women had no one to marry.
⁶⁴ Priests were killed by swords,
    and their widows could not mourn for
      them.

⁶⁵ At last the Lord woke up as though from
    sleep;
    he was like a strong man excited by
      wine.
⁶⁶ He drove his enemies back,
    in lasting and shameful defeat.
⁶⁷ He rejected the descendants of Joseph;
    he did not select the tribe of Ephraim.
⁶⁸ Instead he chose the tribe of Judah,
    and Mount Zion, which he dearly loves.
⁶⁹ There he built his temple,
    like his home in heaven;

he made it firm like the earth,
    secure for all time.

⁷⁰ He chose his servant David;
        he took him from taking care of the
            sheep
⁷¹   and looking after the lambs.
    He made him king of Israel,
        the shepherd of the people of God.
⁷² David took care of them with complete
        devotion
        and led them with skill.

A Prayer for the Nation's Deliverance

79 God, the heathen have invaded your
        people's land!
    They have profaned your holy temple
    and left Jerusalem in ruins.
² They left the bodies of your people for
        birds to eat,
        the bodies of your servants for wild ani-
            mals.
³ They shed your people's blood like water;
        blood flowed like water all over Jeru-
            salem,
        and no one was left to bury the corpses.
⁴ The nations round us make fun of us;
        they laugh at us and mock us.

⁵ How long will you be angry with us, Lord?
        Forever?
    Will your anger continue to burn like
        fire?
⁶ Be angry with the nations that do not wor-
        ship you,
        with the people who reject you!
⁷ They have killed our people
    and ruined our country.

⁸ Do not punish us for the sins of our ances-
        tors,

but have mercy on us now,
because we have lost all hope.
⁹ Help us, God our Saviour,
for the sake of your own honour;
rescue us and forgive our sins,
so that people will praise you.
¹⁰ Why should the nations ask us,
"Where is your God?"
Let us see you punish the nations
for shedding the blood of your servants!

¹¹ Listen to the groans of the prisoners,
and by your great power free those who
are condemned to die.
¹² Lord, pay the other nations back seven
times,
for all the insults they have hurled at
you.
¹³ And we, your people, the sheep of your
flock,
will thank you forever
and praise you for all time to come.

A Prayer for the Nation's Restoration

80 Listen to us, Shepherd of Israel;
hear us, leader of your flock.
Seated on your throne on the cherubim,
² reveal your love for the tribes of
Ephraim, Benjamin, and Manassch!
Show us your strength;
come and save us!

³ Bring us back, God!
Show us your love, and we will be
saved!

⁴ How much longer, Lord God Almighty,
will you be angry with your people's
prayers?
⁵ You have given us tears to eat,
a large cup of tears to drink.

⁶ You let the neighbouring nations fight
over our land,
and our enemies make fun of us.

⁷ Bring us back, Almighty God!
Show us your love, and we will be
saved!

⁸ You brought a grapevine out of Egypt;
you drove out other nations and
planted it in their land.
⁹ You cleared a place for it to grow;
its roots went deep, and it spread out
over the whole land.
¹⁰ It covered the hills with its shade,
the giant cedars with its branches.
¹¹ It extended its branches to the Mediterranean Sea,
and as far as the Euphrates River.
¹² Why did you break down the fences round
it?
Now anyone passing by can steal its
grapes;
¹³   wild pigs trample it down,
and all the wild animals eat it.

¹⁴ Turn to us, Almighty God!
Look down from heaven at us;
come and save your grapevine!
¹⁵ Come and save this vine that you yourself
planted,
this young vine you made grow so
strong!

¹⁶ Our enemies have set it on fire and cut it
down;
look at them in anger and destroy them!
¹⁷ Protect and preserve the people you have
chosen,
the nation you made grow so strong!
¹⁸ We will never turn away from you again;
keep us alive, and we will praise you.

¹⁹ Bring us back, Lord God Almighty!
Show us your love, and we will be
saved!

A Song for a Festival

81 Shout with joy to God our defender;
sing praises to the God of Jacob!
² Start the music and play the tambourines;
play pleasant music on the harps and
the lyres.
³ Blow the horn for the festival;
when the moon is new, and when the
moon is full.
⁴ This is the law in Israel,
an order from the God of Jacob.
⁵ He commanded it to the people of Israel,
when he marched out against the land
of Egypt.

I hear an unfamiliar voice saying,
⁶ "I took the heavy loads off your backs;
I let you put down your workbaskets.
⁷ When you were in trouble you called to
me, and I saved you.
From my hiding place in the storm, I
answered you;
I put you to the test at the springs of
Meribah.

⁸ "Listen, my people, to my warning;
Israel, how I wish you would listen to
me!
⁹ You must never serve a foreign god,
or worship anyone else but me.
¹⁰ I am the Lord, your God,
who brought you out of the land of
Egypt.
Open your mouth, and I will feed you.

¹¹ "But my people would not listen to me;

Israel would not obey me.
12 So I let them go their stubborn ways
    and do whatever they wanted.
13 How I wish my people would listen to me;
    how I wish they would obey me!
14 I would quickly defeat their enemies
    and conquer all their foes.
15 Those who hate me would bow in fear
        before me;
    their punishment would last forever.
16 I would feed you with the finest wheat
    and satisfy you with wild honey."

God the Supreme Ruler

82 God presides in the heavenly council;
    in the meeting of the gods he gives his
        decision:
2 "You must stop judging unjustly,
    and quit being partial to the wicked!
3 Defend the rights of the poor and the
        orphans;
    be fair to the needy and the helpless.
4 Rescue the poor and the needy;
    save them from the power of evil men!

5 "How ignorant you are, how stupid!
    You live in darkness,
    and justice has disappeared from the
        world.
6 I told you that you are gods,
    that all of you are the sons of the Most
        High.
7 But you will die like men;
    your life will end like any prince."

8 Come, God, and rule the world;
    all the nations are yours.

A Prayer for the Defeat of Israel's Enemies

83 God, don't keep silent;
don't be still, God, don't be quiet!
² Look! Your enemies are in revolt,
and those who hate you are rebelling.
³ They are making secret plans against your
people;
they are plotting against those you protect.
⁴ "Come," they say, "let us destroy their
nation,
so that Israel will be forgotten forever!"

⁵ They agree on their plan,
and form an alliance against you:
⁶ the people of Edom, and the Ishmaelites,
the people of Moab, and the Hagrites;
⁷ the people of Gebal, Ammon, and Ama-
lek,
of Philistia and Tyre;
⁸ Assyria has also joined them,
as a strong ally of the descendants of
Lot.

⁹ Do to them what you did to the Midi-
anites,
and to Sisera and Jabin at the Kishon
River,
¹⁰ who were defeated at Endor,
whose bodies rotted on the ground.
¹¹ Do to their generals what you did to Oreb
and Zeeb;
defeat all their rulers as you did Zebah
and Zalmunna
¹² who said, "We will take for our own
the land that belongs to God."

¹³ My God, scatter them like dust,
like straw blown away by the wind.
¹⁴ As the fire burns the forest,
as the flames set the hills on fire,

¹⁵ so chase them away with your storm
and terrify them with your fierce winds.
¹⁶ Cover their faces with shame, Lord,
so they will want to serve you.
¹⁷ May they be defeated and terrified
forever;
may they die in complete disgrace!
¹⁸ May they know that only you are the
Lord,
supreme ruler over all the earth!

Longing for God's House

84 How I love your temple, Almighty
God!
² How I want to be there!
I long for the courts of the Lord's temple.
With my whole being I sing with joy to
the living God.
³ Even the sparrows have built a nest,
and the swallows have their own home;
they keep their young near your altars,
Lord Almighty, my king and my God.
⁴ How happy are those who live in your
temple,
always singing praise to you!

⁵ How happy are those whose strength
comes from you,
who are eager to make the pilgrimage to
Mount Zion.
⁶ As they pass through the dry valley
it becomes a place of springs;
the early rain fills it with pools.
⁷ They grow stronger as they go;
they will see the God of gods on Zion!

⁸ Hear my prayer, Lord God Almighty;
listen, God of Jacob!
⁹ Bless our king, God,
the king you have chosen!

¹⁰ One day spent in your temple
    is better than a thousand anywhere else;
I would rather stand at the gate of the
    house of my God
    than live in the homes of the wicked.
¹¹ The Lord is our protector and glorious
    king,
    blessing us with kindness and honour.
He does not refuse any good thing
    to those who do what is right.
¹² Happy are those who trust in you,
    Almighty God!

A Prayer for the Nation's Welfare

85 Lord, you have been kind to your
    land;
    you made Israel prosperous again.
² You have forgiven your people's sins
    and pardoned all their wrongs.
³ You stopped being angry with them
    and put away your furious rage.

⁴ Bring us back, God our Saviour,
    and stop being displeased with us!
⁵ Will you be angry with us forever?
    Will your anger never cease?
⁶ Please renew our strength,
    and we, your people, will praise you.
⁷ Show us your constant love, Lord,
    and give us your saving help.

⁸ I am listening to what the Lord God is
    saying;
    he promises peace to us, his own peo-
    ple,
    if we do not go back to our foolish ways.
⁹ Surely he is ready to save those who ho-
    nour him,
    and his saving presence will remain in
    our land.

¹⁰ Love and faithfulness will come ᵗ
righteousness and peace will m
¹¹ Man's loyalty will reach up fro
earth,
and God's righteousness will look do
from heaven.
¹² The Lord will make us prosperous,
and our land will produce rich harvests.
¹³ Righteousness will go before the Lord,
and prepare the path for him.

A Prayer for Help

86 Listen to me, Lord, and answer me,
because I am weak and helpless.
² Save me from death, because I am loyal to
you;
save me, because I am your servant and
trust in you.

³ You are my God, so be merciful to me,
Lord;
I pray to you all day long.
⁴ Make your servant glad, Lord,
because my prayers go up to you.
⁵ Lord, you are good and forgiving,
full of constant love for all who pray to
you.

⁶ Listen, Lord, to my prayer;
hear my cries for help.
⁷ I call to you in times of trouble,
because you answer my prayer.

⁸ There is no other god like you, Lord,
not one who can do what you can do.
⁹ All the nations you have created
will come and bow down to you.
They will praise your greatness,
¹⁰ because only you, God, are mighty;
only you do wonderful things.

Teach me, Lord, what you want me to do,
and I will obey you faithfully;
teach me to serve you with complete
devotion.
12 I will praise you with all my heart, Lord
my God;
I will proclaim your greatness forever.
13 How great is your constant love for me!
You have saved me from the depths of
the grave.
14 God, arrogant men are coming against
me;
a gang of cruel men is trying to kill me,
people who pay no attention to you.
15 Lord, you are a merciful and loving God,
slow to anger, always kind and faithful.
16 Turn to me and have mercy on me;
strengthen me and save me,
because I serve you, just as my mother
did.
17 Show me proof of your goodness, Lord,
then those who hate me will be
ashamed,
when they see that you have given me
comfort and help.

In Praise of Jerusalem

87 God built his city on the sacred hills;
2 he loves the city of Jerusalem
more than any other place in Israel.
3 Listen, city of God,
to the wonderful things he says about
you:

4 "When I list the nations that obey me,
I will include Egypt and Babylonia;
and I will say of Philistia, Tyre, and Ethi-
opia,
that they also belong to Jerusalem."
5 Of Zion it will be said
that all nations belong there,

and the Most High will make her
   strong.
⁶ The Lord will write a list of the peoples,
   and include them all as citizens of Jeru-
   alem.
⁷ All who live*ᵐ* there will sing and dance.

A Cry for Help

88   Lord God, my Saviour, I cry out all
        day,
   and at night I come before you.
² Hear my prayer;
   listen to my cry for help!

³ So many troubles have fallen on me
   that I am close to death.
⁴ I am like all others who are about to die;
   all my strength is gone.
⁵ I am abandoned among the dead;
   I am like the slain lying in their graves,
whom you have forgotten completely,
   who are beyond your help.
⁶ You have thrown me into the depths of the
   tomb,
   into the darkest and deepest pit.
⁷ Your anger lies heavy on me,
   and I am crushed beneath its waves.

⁸ You have caused my friends to abandon
   me;
   you have made me repulsive to them.
I am closed in and cannot escape;
⁹   my eyes are weak from suffering.
Lord, every day I call to you,
   and lift my hands to you in prayer!

¹⁰ Do you perform miracles for the dead?
   Do they rise up and praise you?
¹¹ Is your constant love spoken of in the
   grave,

ᵐSome ancient translations who live; *Hebrew* their fountains.

or your faithfulness in the place of destruction?
12 Are your miracles seen in that place of
darkness,
or your goodness in the land of doom?

13 Lord, I call to you for help;
every morning I pray to you.
14 Why do you reject me, Lord?
Why do you hide yourself from me?
15 Ever since I was young I have suffered and
been near death;
I am worn out[n] from the burden of your
punishments.
16 Your furious anger rolls over me;
your terrible attacks destroy me.
17 All day long they surround me like a
flood;
they close in on me from all sides.
18 You have made even my closest friends
abandon me;
darkness is the only companion I have
left.

A Hymn in Time of National Trouble

89 Lord, I will always sing of your constant love;
at all times I will proclaim your faithfulness.
2 I know that your love will last forever,
that your faithfulness is as permanent as
the sky.
3 You said, "I have made a covenant with
the man I chose;
I have promised my servant David,
4 'A descendant of yours will always be
king;
I will preserve your kingdom forever.' "

[n] *Hebrew unclear.*

⁵ The gods in heaven sing of the wonderful
    things you do;
  they sing of your faithfulness, Lord.
⁶ No one in heaven is like you, Lord;
  none of the gods is your equal.
⁷ You are respected in the council of the
    gods,
  and greatly feared by all round you.

⁸ Lord God Almighty, none is as mighty as
    you;
  in all things you are faithful, Lord.
⁹ You rule over the powerful sea;
  you calm its angry waves.
¹⁰ You crushed the monster Rahab and
    killed it;
  with your mighty strength you defeated
    your enemies.
¹¹ The earth is yours, and heaven also;
  you created the world and everything in
    it;
¹² you made the north and the south;
  Mount Tabor and Mount Hermon sing
    to you for joy.
¹³ How powerful you are!
  How great is your strength!
¹⁴ Your kingdom is founded on righteous-
    ness and justice;
  love and faithfulness are in all you do.

¹⁵ Happy are the people who worship you
    with songs,
  who live in the light of your kindness.
¹⁶ Because of you they rejoice all day long
  and praise you because of your good-
    ness.
¹⁷ You give us great victories;
  in your kindness you make us trium-
    phant,
¹⁸ because you chose our protector;
  you, the Holy One of Israel, gave us our
    king.

God's Promise to David

¹⁹ In a vision long ago you said to your faith-
ful servants,
"I have put the crown*o* on a famous
soldier;
I have given the throne to one chosen
from the people.
²⁰ I have selected my servant David
and made him your king.
²¹ My strength will always be with him,
my power will make him strong.
²² His enemies will never succeed against
him,
the wicked will not defeat him.
²³ I will crush his foes
and kill all who hate him.
²⁴ I will always love him and be loyal to him;
I will make him always victorious.
²⁵ I will extend his kingdom
from the Mediterranean Sea to the Euphrates River.
²⁶ He will say to me,
'You are my father and my God;
you are my protector and Saviour.'
²⁷ I will make him my firstborn son,
the greatest of all kings.
²⁸ I will always keep my promise to him,
and my covenant with him will last
forever.
²⁹ A descendant of his will always be king;
his kingdom will be as permanent as the
sky.

³⁰ "But if his descendants disobey my law,
and do not live according to my rules;
³¹ if they disregard my instructions,
and do not keep my commandments,
³² then I will punish them for their sins;
I will whip them for their wrongs.
³³ But I will not stop loving David,

---

*o*crown; *Hebrew* help.

or fail to keep my promise to him.
³⁴ I will not break my covenant with him,
     or take back even one promise I made
          to him.

³⁵ "Once and for all I have promised by my
          holy name:
     I will never lie to David!
³⁶ He will always have descendants,
     and I will watch over his kingdom as
          long as the sun shines.
³⁷ It will be as permanent as the moon,
     as that faithful witness in the sky."

Lament over the Defeat of the King
³⁸ But you are angry with your chosen king;
     you have deserted and rejected him.
³⁹ You have cancelled your covenant with
          your servant,
     and thrown his crown in the dirt.
⁴⁰ You have broken down the walls of his
          city,
     and left his forts in ruins.
⁴¹ All who pass by steal his belongings;
     all his neighbours make fun of him.
⁴² You have given the victory to his enemies;
     you have made them all happy.
⁴³ You have made his weapons useless,
     and let him be defeated in battle.
⁴⁴ You have taken away his royal sceptre,[p]
     and knocked his throne to the ground.
⁴⁵ You have made him old before his time,
     and covered him with disgrace.

A Prayer for Deliverance
⁴⁶ How long will you hide yourself, Lord?
          Forever?
     How long will your anger burn like fire?
⁴⁷ Remember, Lord,[q] how short is man's life;

---

[p]royal sceptre; *Hebrew* purity. [q]Lord; *Hebrew* me.

remember that you created all men
mortal!
⁴⁸ Who can live and never die?
How can man keep himself from the
grave?

⁴⁹ Lord, where are the former proofs of your
love?
Where are the promises you made to
David?
⁵⁰ Don't forget how I, your servant, am insulted;
how I endure all the insults*r* of the heathen.
⁵¹ How your enemies insult your chosen
king, Lord!
They insult him wherever he goes.

⁵² Let us praise the Lord forever!
Amen! Amen!

BOOK FOUR
(Psalms 90–106)

Of God and Man

90 Lord, you have always been our
home.
² Before the hills were created,
before you brought the world into being.
you are eternally God, without beginning or end.

³ You tell men to return to what they were;
you change them back to soil.
⁴ A thousand years to you are like one day;
they are like yesterday, already gone,
like a short hour in the night.

*r*insults; *Hebrew* crowds.

5 You carry men away like a flood;
    they last no longer than a dream.
They are like weeds that sprout in the
    morning,
6   that grow and burst into bloom,
    then dry up and die in the evening.

7 We are destroyed by your anger;
    we are terrified by your fury.
8 You place our sins before you,
    our secret sins where you can see them.

9 Our lifetime is cut short by your anger;
    our life comes to an end like a whisper.
10 Seventy years is all we have—
    eighty years, if we are strong;
    yet all they bring us is worry and trouble;
    life is soon over, and we are gone.

11 Who really knows the full power of your
    anger?
    Who knows what fear your fury can
    bring?
12 Teach us how short our life is,
    so that we may become wise.

13 How long, Lord, before you relent?
    Have pity on your servants!
14 Fill us each morning with your constant
    love,
    that we may sing and be glad all our life.
15 Give us now as much happiness as you
    gave us sadness,
    during all those years when we had
    troubles.
16 Let us, your servants, see your mighty
    acts;
    let our descendants see your glorious
    might.
17 Lord our God, may your blessings be with
    us,

and give us success in all we do!
Yes, give us success in all we do!

God Our Protector

91 Whoever goes to the Most High for
safety,
whoever remains under the protection
of the Almighty,
[2] can say to the Lord,
"You are my defender and protector!
You are my God; in you I trust."

[3] He will surely keep you safe from all hidden dangers,
and from all deadly diseases.
[4] He will cover you with his wings;
you will be safe under his care;
his faithfulness will protect and defend
you.
[5] You will not be afraid of dangers at night,
or of sudden attacks during the day,
[6] of the plagues that strike in the dark,
or of the evils that kill in daylight.

[7] A thousand may fall beside you,
ten thousand all round you,
but you will not be harmed.
[8] You will look and see
how the wicked are punished.

[9] Because you made the Lord your defender,
the Most High your protector,
[10] no disaster will strike you,
no violence will come near your home.
[11] God will put his angels in charge of you,
to protect you wherever you go.
[12] They will hold you up with their hands,
to keep you from hurting your feet on
the rocks.

¹³ You will trample down lions and snakes,
  fierce lions and poisonous snakes.

¹⁴ God says, "I will save those who love me,
  and protect those who know me.
¹⁵ When they call to me, I will answer them;
  when they are in trouble, I will be with
    them.
  I will rescue them and honour them.
¹⁶ I will reward them with long life,
  and will surely save them."

A Song of Praise

92 How good it is to give thanks to the
  Lord,
  to sing in your honour, Most High God,
² to proclaim your constant love every
    morning,
  and your faithfulness every night,
³ with the music of stringed instruments,
  and with melody on the harp.
⁴ Your mighty acts, Lord, make me glad;
  because of what you have done I sing
    for joy.

⁵ How great are your acts, Lord!
  How deep are your thoughts!
⁶ Here is something a fool cannot know,
  a stupid man cannot understand:
⁷ the wicked may grow like weeds,
  and all evildoers may prosper;
  yet they will be totally destroyed,
⁸   because you, Lord, are supreme for-
      ever.

⁹ We know that your enemies will die,
  and all wicked men be defeated.
¹⁰ You have made me as strong as a wild
    bull;
  you have blessed me with happiness.

¹¹ I have seen the defeat of my enemies,
     and heard the cries of the wicked.

¹² The righteous will flourish like palm trees;
     they will grow like the cedars of Leba-
     non.
¹³ They are like trees planted in the house of
     the Lord,
     that flourish in the temple of our God,
¹⁴   that still bear fruit in old age,
     and are always green and strong.
¹⁵ This shows that the Lord is just;
     in him, my defender, there is no wrong.

God the King

93   The Lord is king!
     He is clothed with majesty,
   and covered with strength.
Surely the earth is set firmly in place
   and cannot be moved.
² Your throne, Lord, has been firm from the
     beginning,
     and you existed before time began.

³ The ocean depths raise their voice, Lord;
     they raise their voice and roar.
⁴ The Lord rules supreme in heaven,
     greater than the roar of the ocean,
     more powerful than the waves of the
     sea.

⁵ Your laws are eternal, Lord,
     and your temple is holy indeed,
     forever and ever.

God the Judge of All

94   Lord, you are a God who punishes;
     reveal[s] your anger!
² You are the judge of all men;

[s]Some ancient translations reveal; *Hebrew* you revealed.

rise and give the proud what they deserve!

3 How much longer will the wicked be glad?
How much longer, Lord?

4 How much longer will evildoers be proud
and boast about their crimes?

5 They crush your people, Lord;
they oppress those who belong to you.

6 They kill widows and orphans,
and murder the strangers who live in
our land.

7 They say, "The Lord doesn't see us;
the God of Israel does not notice!"

8 My people, how can you be such stupid
fools?
When will you ever learn?

9 God made our ears—can't he hear?
He made our eyes—can't he see?

10 He is in charge of the nations—won't he
punish them?
He is the teacher of all men—doesn't he
know?

11 The Lord knows what they think;
he knows how senseless their reasoning
is.

12 Lord, happy is the man whom you instruct,
the man to whom you teach your law,

13 to give him rest from days of trouble,
until a grave is dug for the wicked.

14 The Lord will not abandon his people;
he will not desert those who belong to
him.

15 Justice will again be found in courts of
judgement,
and all righteous people will support it.

16 Who stood up for me against the wicked?
Who took my side against the evildoers?

¹⁷ If the Lord had not helped me,
    I would have gone quickly to the land
      of silence.
¹⁸ I said, "I am falling";
    but, Lord, your constant love held me
      up.
¹⁹ When I am anxious and worried,
    you comfort me and make me glad.

²⁰ You have nothing to do with corrupt
    judges,
    who make injustice legal,
²¹ who plot against good men,
    and sentence the innocent to death.
²² But the Lord defends me;
    my God protects me.
²³ He will punish them for their wickedness,
    and destroy them for their sins;
    the Lord our God will destroy them.

A Song of Praise

95   Come, let us praise the Lord!
    Let us sing for joy to our protector
      and Saviour!
² Let us come before him with thanksgiv-
    ing,
    and sing joyful songs of praise!
³ For the Lord is a mighty God,
    a mighty king over all the gods.
⁴ He rules over the whole earth,
    from the deepest caves to the highest
      hills.
⁵ He rules over the sea, which he made;
    the land also, which he himself formed.

⁶ Come, let us bow down and worship him;
    let us kneel before the Lord, our Maker!
⁷ He is our God;
    we are the people he looks after,
    the flock for which he provides.

Let us praise the Lord!

Listen today to what he says:
8 "Don't be stubborn, as your ancestors
      were at Meribah,
      as they were that day in the desert at
      Massah.
9 There they put me to the test and tried
      me,
      although they had seen what I did for
      them.
10 For forty years I was disgusted with those
      people;
      I said, 'How disloyal they are!
      They refuse to obey my commands!'

¹¹ I was angry and made a solemn promise,
'You will never enter the land where I,
would give you rest.' "

God the Supreme King

96 Sing a new song to the Lord!
Sing to the Lord, all the world!
² Sing to the Lord, and praise him!
Every day tell the good news that he
has saved us!
³ Proclaim his glory to the nations,
his mighty acts to all peoples.

⁴ The Lord is great, and must be highly
praised;
he must be feared more than all the
gods.
⁵ The gods of all other nations are only
idols,
but the Lord made the heavens.
⁶ Glory and majesty are round him,
greatness and beauty are in his temple.

⁷ All people on earth, praise the Lord!
Praise his glory and might!
⁸ Praise the Lord's glorious name;
bring an offering and come into his temple.
⁹ Bow down before the Holy One when he
appears;
tremble before him, all the earth!

¹⁰ Say to all the nations, "The Lord is king!
The earth is set firmly in place and can-
not be moved;
he will judge all peoples with justice."
¹¹ Be glad, earth and sky!
Roar, sea, and all the creatures in you;
¹² be glad, fields, and everything in you!
Then the trees in the woods will shout for
joy before the Lord,

¹³ because he comes to rule the earth.
   He will rule all peoples of the world
      with justice and fairness.

God the Supreme Ruler

97 The Lord is king! Be glad, earth!
      Rejoice, all you islands of the
         seas!
² Clouds and darkness are round him;
   his kingdom is based on righteousness
      and justice.
³ Fire goes in front of him,
   and burns up his enemies round him.
⁴ His lightning lights up the world;
   the earth sees it and trembles.
⁵ The hills melt like wax before the Lord,
   before the Lord of all the earth.
⁶ The heavens proclaim his righteousness,
   and all peoples see his glory.

⁷ All who worship images are ashamed,
   all who boast of their idols;
   all the gods bow down before him.
⁸ The people of Zion are glad,
   and the cities of Judah rejoice,
      because of your judgements, Lord!
⁹ Lord Almighty, you are ruler of all the
      earth;
   you are much greater than all the gods.

¹⁰ The Lord loves those who hate evil;^t
   he protects the lives of his people,
   he rescues them from the power of the
      wicked.
¹¹ Light shines on the righteous,
   and gladness on the good.
¹² All you that are righteous, be glad,
   because of what the Lord has done!

The Lord loves those who hate evil; *Hebrew* Hate evil, you who love
the Lord.

Remember what the Holy One has done,
and give thanks to him!

God the Ruler of the World

98 Sing a new song to the Lord;
he has done wonderful things!
By his own power and holy strength,
he has won the victory.
2 The Lord announced his victory;
he made his saving power known to the
nations.
3 He kept his promise to the people of
Israel,
with constant love and loyalty for them.
All people everywhere have seen the victory of our God!

4 Sing for joy to the Lord, all the earth;
praise him with songs and shouts of joy!
5 Sing praises to the Lord with harps;
play music on the harps!
6 With trumpets and horns,
shout for joy before the Lord, the king!

7 Roar, sea, and all creatures in you;
sing, earth, and all who live there!
8 Clap your hands, oceans;
hills, sing together with joy before the
Lord,
9 because he comes to rule the earth!
He will rule all peoples of the world
with justice and fairness.

God the Supreme King

99 The Lord is king;
the people tremble;
he sits on his throne on the cherubim;
the earth shakes.
2 The Lord is mighty in Zion;
he rules over all the nations.

³ Everyone will praise his great and majestic name.
Holy is he!

⁴ Mighty king,ᵘ you love what is right;
you have brought justice to Israel;
you have brought righteousness and
fairness.
⁵ Praise the Lord our God;
worship before his throne!
Holy is he!

⁶ Moses and Aaron were his priests,
and Samuel was one who worshipped
him;
they called to the Lord and he answered
them.
⁷ He spoke to them from the column of
cloud;
they obeyed the laws and commandments that he gave them.

⁸ Lord, our God, you answered your people;
you showed them that you are a God
who forgives,
but you punished them for their sins,
⁹ Praise the Lord our God
and worship at his sacred mountain!
The Lord our God is holy!

A Hymn of Praise

100 Sing for joy to the Lord, all the
world!
² Worship the Lord gladly,
and come before him with joyful songs!

³ Never forget that the Lord is God!
He made us, and we belong to him;
we are his people, we are his flock.

ᵘMighty king; *Hebrew* The might of the king.

⁴ Enter his temple with thanksgiving,
    go into his sanctuary with praise!
    Give thanks to him and praise him!

⁵ The Lord is good;
    his love lasts forever,
    and his faithfulness for all time.

A King's Promise

101 My song is about loyalty and jus-
        tice,
    and I sing it to you, Lord.
² My conduct will be faultless.
    When will you come to me?

    I will live a pure life in my house;
³   I will never tolerate evil.

    I hate the actions of those who turn away
            from God;
        I will have nothing to do with them.
⁴ I will not be dishonest;
    I will not even think of evil.

⁵ I will destroy a man
    who whispers evil things about his
            friend;
    I will not tolerate a man
    who is proud and arrogant.

⁶ I will approve of those who are faithful to
            God,
    and let them live in my palace;
    those who are completely honest
    will be allowed to serve me.

⁷ No liar will live in my palace;
    no hypocrite will remain in my pres-
            ence.

⁸ Day after day I will destroy
    all the wicked in our land;

I will expel all evil men
 from the city of the Lord.

The Prayer of a Troubled Man[v]

102 Listen to my prayer, Lord,
  and hear my cry for help!
2 Don't hide yourself from me
 when I am in trouble!
Listen to me,
 and answer me quickly when I call!

3 My life disappears like smoke;
 my body burns like fire.
4 I am beaten down like dry grass;
 I have lost my desire for food.
5 I groan aloud;
 I am nothing but skin and bones.
6 I am like a wild bird in the desert,
 like an owl in abandoned ruins.
7 I lie awake;
 I am like a lonely bird on a housetop.
8 All day long my enemies insult me;
 those who make fun of me use my name
  in cursing.

9 Ashes are my food,
 and my tears are mixed with my drink,
10 because of your anger and fury.
You picked me up and threw me away.
11 My life is like the evening shadows;
 I am like dry grass.

12 But you, Lord, are king forever;
 all generations will remember you.
13 You will rise and take pity on Zion;
 the time has come to have mercy on
  her;

[v]*Hebrew title:* The prayer of a man in trouble who in distress pours
out his complaint to the Lord.

this is the right time!

14 Your servants love her, even though she is
destroyed;

they have pity on her, even though she
is in ruins.

15 The nations will fear the Lord;
all the kings of the earth will fear his
power.

16 When the Lord rebuilds Zion,
he will reveal his greatness.

17 He will hear his abandoned people
and listen to their prayer.

18 Write down for the coming generation
what the Lord did,
so that people not yet born will praise
him.

19 The Lord looked down from his holy
place on high,
he looked down from heaven to the
earth,

20 to hear the groans of prisoners,
and to set free those who were condemned to die.

21 And so men will proclaim the name of the
Lord in Zion;
they will give thanks to him in Jerusalem,

22 when nations and kingdoms come
together
and worship the Lord.

23 The Lord made me weak while I was still
young;
he has shortened my life.

24 My God, do not take me away now,
before I grow old!

Lord, you live forever;

25 long ago you created the earth,
and with your own hands you made the
heavens.

²⁶ They will all disappear, but you will remain;
    they will all wear out like clothes.
  You will change them like clothes, and
    they will vanish;
²⁷   but you are always the same, and your
      life never ends.
²⁸ Our children will live in safety,
    and their descendants will always live
      under your protection.

The Love of God

103 Praise the Lord, my soul!
      All my being, praise his holy
        name!
² Praise the Lord, my soul,
    and do not forget how kind he is.
³ He forgives all my sins
    and heals all my diseases;
⁴ he saves me from the grave
    and blesses me with love and mercy;
⁵ he fills my life ʷ with good things,
    so that I stay young and strong like an
      eagle.

⁶ The Lord judges in favour of the op-
    pressed
    and gives them their rights.
⁷ He told his plans to Moses
    and let the people of Israel see his
      mighty acts.
⁸ The Lord is merciful and loving,
    slow to become angry, and full of con-
      stant love.
⁹ He does not keep on reprimanding;
    he is not angry forever.
¹⁰ He does not punish us as we deserve,
    or repay us for our sins and wrongs.
¹¹ As high as the sky is above the earth,
    so great is his love for those who fear
      him.

ʷmy life; *Hebrew unclear.*

¹² As far as the east is from the west,
   so far does he remove our sins from us.
¹³ As kind as a father is to his children,
   so the Lord is kind to those who fear
      him.
¹⁴ He knows what we are made of;
   he remembers that we are dust.

The wind blows on it, and it is gone

¹⁵ As for man, his life is like grass;
    he grows and flourishes like a wild
        flower.
¹⁶ Then the wind blows on it, and it is gone,
    and no one sees it again.
¹⁷ But the Lord's love for those who honour
        him lasts forever,
    and his goodness endures for all genera-
        tions,
¹⁸ to those who are true to his covenant,
    and who faithfully obey his command-
        ments.

¹⁹ The Lord set up his throne in heaven;
    he is king over all.
²⁰ Praise the Lord, you strong and mighty
        angels,
    who obey his commands,
    who listen to what he says!
²¹ Praise the Lord, all you heavenly powers,
    you servants who do what he wants!
²² Praise the Lord, all his creatures,
    in every place he rules!
    Praise the Lord, my soul!

In Praise of the Creator

104 Praise the Lord, my soul!
    Lord, my God, how great you
        are!
You are clothed with majesty and glory;
²   you cover yourself with light.
You stretched out the heavens like a tent,
³   and built your home on the waters
        above.
You use the clouds as your chariot,
    and walk on the wings of the wind.
⁴ You use the winds as your messengers,
    and flashes of lightning as your serv-
        ants.

⁵ You have set the earth firmly on its foun-
        dations,

and it will never be moved.
⁶ You placed the ocean over it like a robe,
  and the water covered the mountains;
⁷ but when you reprimanded the waters,
    they fled;
  when they heard your shout of com-
    mand, they rushed away.
⁸ They went over the mountains down into
    the valleys,
  to the place you had made for them;
⁹ you set a boundary they can never pass,
  to keep them from covering the earth
    again.

¹⁰ You make springs flow in the valleys,
  and water run between the hills.
¹¹ They provide water for the wild animals;
  the wild donkeys quench their thirst;
¹² in the trees near by
  the birds make their nests and sing.

¹³ From heaven you send rain on the moun-
    tains,
  and the earth is filled with your bless-
    ings.
¹⁴ You make grass grow for the cattle,
  and plants for man to use,
  so he can grow his crops,
¹⁵   and produce wine to make him happy,
  olive oil to make him cheerful,
  and bread to give him strength.

¹⁶ The cedars of Lebanon get plenty of rain,
  the Lord's own trees, which he planted.
¹⁷ There the birds build their nests;
  the storks nest in the fir trees.
¹⁸ The wild goats live in the high mountains,
  and the badgers hide in the cliffs.

¹⁹ You created the moon to mark the
    months;
  the sun knows the time to set.

You make springs flow in the valley

²⁰ You made the night, and in the darkness
all the wild animals come out.
²¹ The young lions roar while they hunt,
looking for the food that God gives
them.
²² When the sun rises they go back
and lie down in their dens.
²³ Then men go out to do their work,
and keep working until evening.

²⁴ Lord, you have made so many things!
How wisely you made them all!
The earth is filled with your creatures.
²⁵ There is the ocean, large and wide,
where countless creatures live,
large and small alike;
²⁶ the ships sail on it, and Leviathan plays in
it,
that sea monster which you made.

²⁷ All of them depend on you,
to give them food when they need it.
²⁸ You give it to them, and they eat it;
you provide food, and they are satisfied.
²⁹ When you turn away, they are afraid;
when you hold back your breath, they
die,
and go back to the soil they came from.
³⁰ But when you give them breath, they live;
you give new life to the earth.

³¹ May the glory of the Lord last forever!
May the Lord be happy with what he
made!
³² He looks at the earth, and it trembles;
he touches the mountains, and they
pour out smoke.

³³ I will sing to the Lord all my life;
I will sing praises to my God as long as
I live.
³⁴ May he be pleased with my song,

because he makes me glad..
³⁵ May sinners be destroyed from the earth;
    may the wicked be no more!

Praise the Lord, my soul!
Praise the Lord!

God and His People

105 Give thanks to the Lord, proclaim
        his greatness,
    and make known to the nations what he
        has done!
² Sing to him, sing praise to him;
    tell all the wonderful things he has
        done!
³ Be glad that we belong to him;
    let all who serve the Lord rejoice!
⁴ Go to the Lord for help;
    stay in his presence always.
⁵⁻⁶ You descendants of Abraham, his servant,
    you descendants of Jacob, his chosen
        one:
    remember his great and wonderful mira-
        cles,
    and the judgements he gave.

⁷ He, the Lord, is our God;
    his commands are for all the world.
⁸ He will keep his covenant forever,
    his promises for a thousand genera-
        tions,
⁹ the agreement he made with Abraham,
    and his promise to Isaac.
¹⁰ The Lord made an eternal covenant with
        Israel,
    a lasting agreement with Jacob, when
        he said,
¹¹ "I will give you the land of Canaan;
    it will be your own possession."

¹² God's people were few in number,

and they were strangers in the land.
13 They wandered from country to country,
from one kingdom to another,
14 but he did not let anyone oppress them,
and he reprimanded kings on their account.
15 He said, "Don't touch my chosen servants;
do not harm my prophets!"

16 When the Lord sent famine to their country,
and took away all their food,
17 he sent Joseph ahead of them,
who had been sold as a slave.
18 His feet were hurt by tight chains,
and an iron collar was put round his neck,
19 until what he had predicted came true.
The word of the Lord proved him right.
20 Then the king of Egypt had him released;
the ruler of nations set him free.
21 He put him in charge of his government,
and made him ruler over all the land,
22 with complete authority over the king's officials,
and power to instruct his advisers.

23 Then Jacob went to Egypt,
and settled in that country.
24 The Lord let his people have many children,
and made them stronger than their enemies.
25 He made the Egyptians hate his people,
and act deceitfully with his servants.

26 Then he sent his servant Moses,
and Aaron, whom he chose.
27 They did God's mighty acts,
and performed miracles in Egypt.
28 He sent darkness on the land,

but the Egyptians did not obey[x] his
    command.

29 He turned their rivers into blood,
    and killed all their fish.

30 Their country was filled with frogs,
    even the king's palace.

31 God commanded, and flies and gnats
    filled the whole country.

32 He sent hail and lightning on their land,
    instead of rain;

33 he destroyed their grapevines and fig
    trees,
    and broke down the trees.

34 He commanded, and the grasshoppers
    came,
    countless millions of them;

35 they ate all the plants in the land;
    they ate all the crops.

36 He killed the firstborn sons
    of all the families of Egypt.

37 Then he led the Israelites out;
    they carried silver and gold,
    and all of them were strong and
    healthy.

38 The Egyptians were glad when they left,
    because they were afraid of them.

39 He put a cloud over his people
    and a fire to give them light by night.

40 They[y] asked, and he sent quails,
    he gave them food from heaven to sat-
    isfy them.

41 He opened a rock, and water gushed out,
    flowing through the desert like a river.

42 He remembered his sacred promise
    to Abraham his servant.

43 So he led his people out with singing,
    his chosen people with shouts of joy.

44 He gave them the lands of foreigners,

---

[x]Some ancient translations did not obey; Hebrew obeyed. [y]Some ancient translations They; Hebrew He.

t them take over their fields,
      his people would obey his laws,
   id keep his commandments.

Praise the Lord!

The Lord's Goodness to His People

106 Praise the Lord!

Give thanks to the Lord, because he is
      good;
   his love is eternal.
2 Who can tell all the great things he has
      done?
   Who can praise him enough?
3 Happy are those who obey his command,
   who always do what is right!

4 Remember me, Lord, when you help your
      people;
   include me, when you save them.
5 Let me see the prosperity of your people,
   and share in the happiness of your na-
      tion,
   in the glad pride of those who belong to
      you.

6 We have sinned, as our ancestors did;
   we have been wicked and evil.
7 Our ancestors in Egypt did not under-
      stand God's wonderful acts;
   they forgot the many times he showed
      his love for them,
   and they rebelled against the Almighty[z]
      at the Sea of Reeds.
8 But he saved them, as he had promised,
   in order to show his great power.
9 He commanded the Sea of Reeds, and it
      dried up,

zthe Almighty; *Hebrew* against the sea.

and he led his people across it as though
    on dry land.

10 He saved them from those who hated
    them;
    he rescued them from their enemies.

11 The water drowned their enemies;
    not one of them was left.

12 Then his people believed his promises,
    and sang praise to him.

13 But they quickly forgot what he had done,
    and acted without waiting for his ad-
    vice.

14 They were filled with desire in the desert,
    and put God to the test;

15 so he gave them what they asked for,
    but sent a terrible disease among them.

16 There in the desert they were jealous of
    Moses,
    and of Aaron, the Lord's holy servant;

17 then the earth opened up and swallowed
    Dathan,
    and buried Abiram and his family;

18 fire came down on their followers,
    and burned up those wicked people.

19 They made a gold calf at Horeb,
    and worshipped this image;

20 they exchanged the glory of God
    for the image of an animal that eats
    grass.

21 They forgot the God who had saved them,
    by his mighty acts in Egypt.

22 What wonderful things he did there!
    What amazing things he did at the Sea
    of Reeds!

23 And so God said he would destroy his
    people;
    but Moses, his chosen servant, stood up
    against God,
    and kept his anger from destroying
    them.

²⁴ Then they refused the pleasant land,
  because they did not believe God's
  promise.
²⁵ They stayed in their tents and grumbled,
  and would not listen to the Lord.
²⁶ So he gave them a solemn warning
  that he would make them die in the
  desert,
²⁷ and scatter their descendants among the
  heathen,
  letting them die in foreign countries.

²⁸ Then God's people joined in the worship
  of Baal, at Peor,
  and ate the sacrifices offered to dead
  gods.
²⁹ They stirred up the Lord's anger by their
  actions,
  and a terrible disease broke out among
  them;
³⁰ but Phinehas stood up and punished the
  guilty,
  and the plague was stopped,
³¹ and this has been remembered in his favour ever since,
  and will be for all time to come.

³² The Lord's people made him angry at the
  springs of Meribah,
  and Moses was in trouble on their account.
³³ They made Moses so bitter,
  that he said things he shouldn't have
  said.

³⁴ They did not kill the heathen,
  as the Lord had commanded,
³⁵ but intermarried with them,
  and imitated their pagan ways.
³⁶ God's people worshipped idols,
  and this caused their destruction.
³⁷ They offered their own sons and daughters

as sacrifices to pagan gods;
³⁸ they killed these innocent people,
their own sons and daughters,
as a sacrifice to the idols of Canaan;
the land was made impure by these kill-
ings.
³⁹ They defiled themselves by their actions,
and were unfaithful to God.

⁴⁰ So the Lord was angry with his people;
he was disgusted with them.
⁴¹ He abandoned them to the power of the
heathen,
and their enemies ruled over them.
⁴² They were oppressed by their enemies,
and were in complete subjection to
them.
⁴³ Many times the Lord rescued his people,
but they chose to rebel against him,
and sank deeper into sin,
⁴⁴ Yet the Lord heard them when they cried
out,
and took notice of their distress.
⁴⁵ For their sake he remembered his cove-
nant,
and because of his great love he
changed his mind.
⁴⁶ He made those who held them prisoners
feel sorry for them.

⁴⁷ Save us, Lord our God,
and bring us back from among the nations,
so that we may praise your holy name,
and be happy in thanking you.

⁴⁸ Let us praise the Lord, the God of Israel;
praise him now and forever!
All the people are to say, "Amen!"

Praise the Lord!

BOOK FIVE
(Psalms 107–150)

In Praise of God's Goodness

107 Give thanks to the Lord, because
                  he is good;
  his love is eternal!
2 Join me in praising the Lord,
    all you whom he has saved.
He has rescued you from your enemies,
3   and brought you back from foreign
       countries,
    from east and west, from north and
       south.*a*

4 Some wandered in the trackless desert,
    and could not find their way to a city to
       live in;
5 they were hungry and thirsty,
    and had given up all hope.
6 In their trouble they called to the Lord,
    and he saved them from their distress.
7 He led them out,
    straight to a city to live in.
8 They must thank the Lord for his constant
       love,
    for the wonderful things he did for
       them!
9 He satisfies those who are thirsty,
    and the hungry he fills with good things.

10 Some were living in gloom and darkness,
    prisoners suffering in chains,
11 because they had rebelled against the
       commands of Almighty God,
    and had rejected his instructions.
12 They were worn out from hard work;

*a*south; *Hebrew* the sea (*meaning* "west").

they would fall down, and no one would
help.

13 In their trouble they called to the Lord,
and he saved them from their distress.
14 He brought them out of their gloom and
darkness,
and smashed their chains.
.15 They must thank the Lord for his constant
love,
for the wonderful things he did for
them.
16 He breaks down bronze doors,
and smashes iron bars.

17 Some were sick[b] because of their sins,
suffering because of their evil;
18 they couldn't stand the sight of food,
and were close to dying.
19 In their trouble they called to the Lord,
and he saved them from their distress.
20 He healed them with his command,
and saved them from the grave.
21 They must thank the Lord for his constant
love,
for the wonderful things he did for
them.
22 They must thank him with sacrifices,
and with songs of joy tell all he has
done!

23 Some sailed over the ocean in ships,
earning their living on the seas;
24 they saw what the Lord has done,
his wonderful acts on the seas.
25 He commanded, and a mighty wind began
to blow
and stirred up the waves.
26 The ships were lifted high in the air and
plunged down into the depths;
in such danger, the men lost their courage;

[b]sick; *Hebrew* fools.

²⁷ they stumbled and staggered like drunken
  men;
  all their skill was useless.
²⁸ In their trouble they called to the Lord,
  and he saved them from their distress.
²⁹ He made the storm be still,
  and the waves became quiet.
³⁰ They were glad because of the calm,
  and he brought them safe to the port
  they wanted.

And he brought them safe to the port

³¹ They must thank the Lord for his constant
  love,
  for the wonderful things he did for
  them.
³² They must proclaim his greatness in the
  assembly of the people,
  and praise him before the council of the
  elders.

³³ The Lord has made rivers dry up com-
  pletely,
  and stopped springs from flowing.
³⁴ He has made rich soil become a salty
  wasteland,
  because of the wickedness of those who
  lived there.

³⁵ He has changed deserts into pools of water,
    and dry land into flowing springs.
³⁶ He has let hungry people settle there,
    and they built a city to live in;
³⁷ they sowed the fields and planted grapevines,
    which produced an abundant harvest.
³⁸ He blessed his people and they had many children,
    and he kept their herds of cattle from decreasing.

³⁹ When God's people were defeated and humiliated,
    by cruel oppression and suffering,
⁴⁰ he showed his contempt for their oppressors,
    and made them wander in the trackless deserts.
⁴¹ But he rescued the needy from their misery,
    and made their families increase like flocks.
⁴² The righteous see this, and are glad,
    but all the wicked are put to silence.

⁴³ May those who are wise think about these things;
    may they acknowledge the Lord's constant love.

A Prayer for Help against Enemies

(Psalms 57.7–11; 60.5–12)

108 I am ready, God;
    I am completely ready!
I will sing and praise you!
Wake up, my soul!
² Wake up, my harp and lyre!
I will wake up the sun!

³ I will thank you among the nations, Lord!
  I will praise you among the peoples!
⁴ Your constant love reaches above the
      heavens,
  your faithfulness to the skies.

⁵ God, show your greatness in the sky,
  and your glory over all the earth!
⁶ Save us by your might; answer my prayer,
  so that the people you love may be res-
      cued.

⁷ In his sanctuary God has said,
      "In triumph I will divide Shechem,
      and distribute Succoth Valley to my
          people.
⁸ Gilead is mine, and Manasseh too;
      Ephraim is my helmet,
      and Judah my royal sceptre.
⁹ But I will use Moab as my washbowl
      and Edom as my sandal box.
      I will shout in triumph over Philistia."

¹⁰ Who will take me, God, into the fortified
      city?
      Who will bring me to Edom?
¹¹ Have you really rejected us?
      Aren't you going to march out with our
          armies?
¹² Help us fight the enemy,
      because human help is worthless!
¹³ With God on our side we will win;
      he will defeat our enemies.

The Complaint of a Man in Trouble

109 I praise you, God; don't be silent!
      ² Wicked men and liars have at-
          tacked me,
  telling lies about me.
³ They say terrible things about me,
  attacking me for no reason.

⁴They oppose me, even though I love them,
 and have prayed for them.
⁵They pay me back evil for good,
 and hatred for love.

⁶Choose a corrupt man to judge my enemy,
 and let one of his own enemies accuse him.
⁷May he be tried and found guilty;
 may even his prayer be considered a crime!
⁸May his life soon be ended;
 may another man take his job!
⁹May his children become orphans,
 and his wife a widow!
¹⁰May his children be homeless beggars;
 may they be driven from*c* the ruins they live in!
¹¹May his creditors take away all his property,
 and strangers get everything he worked for.
¹²May no one ever be kind to him;
 may no one take care of his orphans.
¹³May all his descendants die,
 and his name be forgotten in the next generation.
¹⁴May the Lord remember the evil of his ancestors,
 and never forgive his mother's sins.
¹⁵May the Lord always remember their sins,
 but may they themselves be completely forgotten!
¹⁶That man never thought of being kind;
 the poor, the needy, and the helpless
 he persecuted and killed.
¹⁷He loved to curse—may he be cursed!
 He hated to bless—may no one bless him!
¹⁸He cursed as easily as he dressed himself;

cOne ancient translation be driven from; *Hebrew* seek.

may his curses soak into him like water,
and soak into his bones like oil!
19 May they cover him like clothes,
and be always round him like a belt.

20 May this be how the Lord punishes my
enemies,
who say such terrible things against me!
21 But Lord, my God, help me as you have
promised,
and rescue me because of the goodness
of your love.
22 I am poor and needy;
I am hurt to the depths of my heart.
23 I am about to vanish like an evening
shadow;
I am blown away like an insect.
24 My knees are weak from lack of food;
my body is thin and feeble.
25 When people see me, they make fun of
me;
they shake their heads in scorn.

26 Help me, Lord my God;
save me because of your constant love!
27 Make my enemies know
that you are the one who saves me.
28 They may curse me, but you will bless me.
May my persecutors be defeated,*d*
and may I, your servant, be glad.
29 May my enemies be covered with disgrace;
may they wear their shame like a robe.

30 I will give loud thanks to the Lord;
I will praise him in the meeting of the
people,
31 because he defends the poor man,
to save him from those who condemn
him to death.

---

d One ancient translation May my persecutors be defeated; *Hebrew*
They persecuted me and were defeated.

The Lord and His Chosen King

110 The Lord said to my lord, the king,
"Sit here at my right side,
until I put your enemies under your
feet."
2 From Zion the Lord will extend your
royal power.
"Rule over your enemies," he says.
3 The day you fight your enemies
your people will volunteer.
Like the dew early in the morning,
your young men will come to you on
the sacred hills.*e*

4 The Lord made a solemn promise, and
will not take it back:
"You will be a priest forever,
in the priestly order of Melchizedek."

5 The Lord is at your right side;
he will defeat kings on the day he
becomes angry.
6 He will pass judgement on the nations,
and fill the battlefield with corpses;
he will defeat kings over the whole
earth.
7 The king will drink from the stream by the
road,
and strengthened, he will stand victorious.

In Praise of the Lord

111 Praise the Lord!

With all my heart I will thank the Lord,
in the meeting of his people.
2 How wonderful are the things the Lord
does!
All who are pleased with them want to
understand them.

e Hebrew text uncertain and unclear.

³ All he does is full of honour and majesty;
    his righteousness is eternal.

⁴ The Lord does not let us forget his won-
        derful actions;
    he is kind and merciful.
⁵ He provides food for those who fear him;
    he never forgets his covenant.
⁶ He has shown his power to his people,
    by giving them the lands of foreigners.

⁷ In all he does he is faithful and just;
    all his commandments are dependable.
⁸ They last for all time;
    they were given in truth and righteous-
        ness.
⁹ He brought salvation to his people,
    and made an eternal covenant with
        them.
    Holy and mighty is he!
¹⁰ The way to become wise is to fear the
        Lord;
    he gives sound judgement to all who
        obey his commands.
    He is to be praised forever!

The Happiness of a Good Person

112 Praise the Lord!

Happy is the man who fears the
        Lord,
    who takes pleasure in obeying
        his commands.
² His children will be mighty in the land;
    the good man's descendants will be
        blessed.
³ His family will be wealthy and rich,
    and he will be prosperous forever.

⁴ Light shines in the darkness for good men,
    for those who are kind, merciful, and
        just.

⁵ Happy is the man who is generous in his
  loans,
  who runs his business honestly.
⁶ A good man will never fail;
  he will never be forgotten.

⁷ He is not afraid of receiving bad news;
  his faith is strong, and he trusts in the
  Lord.
⁸ He is not worried or afraid;
  he is certain he will see his enemies defeated.
⁹ He gives generously to the needy,
  and his kindness is eternal;
  he will be powerful and respected.
¹⁰ The wicked see this and are upset;
  they glare in anger and disappear;
  their hopes are gone forever.

In Praise of the Lord's Goodness

113 Praise the Lord!

You servants of the Lord,
  praise his name!
² His name will be praised,
  now and forever!
³ From the east to the west,
  the Lord's name be praised!
⁴ The Lord rules over all nations,
  his glory is above the heavens.

⁵ There is no one like the Lord our God;
  he lives in the heights above,
⁶ but he bends down
  to see the heavens and the earth.
⁷ He raises the poor from the dust;
  he lifts the needy from their misery,
⁸ and makes them companions of princes,
  the princes of his people.
⁹ He honours the childless wife in her
  home;

he makes her happy by giving her children.

Praise the Lord!

A Passover Song

114 When the people of Israel left
       Egypt,
   when Jacob's descendants left that foreign land,
² Judah became the Lord's holy people,
   Israel became his own possession.

³ The Sea of Reeds looked and ran away,
   the Jordan River stopped flowing.
⁴ The mountains skipped like goats,
   the hills skipped around like sheep.

⁵ What happened, Sea, to make you run
       away?
   And you, Jordan, why did you stop
       flowing?
⁶ Mountains, why did you skip like goats?
   Hills, why did you skip around like
       sheep?

⁷ Tremble, earth, at the Lord's coming,
   at the presence of the God of Jacob,
⁸ who changes rocks into pools of water,
   and stone cliffs into flowing springs.

The One True God

115 To you alone, Lord, to you alone,
       and not to us, must glory be
       given,
   because of your constant love and faithfulness.

2 Why should the nations ask us,
   "Where is your God?"
3 Our God is in heaven,
   doing whatever he wishes.
4 Their gods are made of silver and gold,
   formed by human hands.
5 They have mouths, but cannot speak,
   and eyes, but cannot see.
6 They have ears, but cannot hear,
   and noses, but cannot smell.
7 They have hands, but cannot feel,
   and feet, but cannot walk;
   they cannot make a sound.
8 May those who made them and all who
     trust in them,
   become like the idols they have made!

9 Trust in the Lord, people of Israel!
   He helps you and protects you.
10 Trust in the Lord, you priests of God!
   He helps you and protects you.
11 Trust in the Lord, all who fear him!
   He helps you and protects you.

12 The Lord remembers us and will bless us;
   he will bless the people of Israel,
   and all the priests of God.
13 He will bless all who fear him,
   the great and the small alike.

14 May the Lord give you children
   you and your descendants.
15 May you be blessed by the Lord,
   who made heaven and earth!

16 Heaven belongs to the Lord alone,
   but he gave the earth to men.
17 The Lord is not praised by the dead,
   by any who go down to the land of
     silence.

¹⁸ But we, the living, will give thanks to him,
   now and forever.

Praise the Lord!

A Man Saved from Death Praises God

116 I love the Lord, because he hears
   me;
   he listens to my prayers.
² He listens to me
   every time I call to him.
³ Death drew its ropes tight round me,
   the horrors of the grave closed in on
   me;
   I was filled with fear and anxiety.
⁴ Then I called to the Lord,
   "I beg you, Lord, save me!"

⁵ The Lord is merciful and good;
   our God is compassionate.
⁶ The Lord protects the helpless;
   when I was in danger, he saved me.
⁷ Be confident, my heart,
   because the Lord has been good to me.

⁸ The Lord has saved me from death;
   he stopped my tears
   and kept me from defeat.
⁹ And so I walk in the presence of the Lord
   in the world of the living.
¹⁰ I kept on believing, even when I said,
   "I am completely crushed,"
¹¹ even when I was afraid and said,
   "No one can be trusted."

¹² What can I offer the Lord
   for all his goodness to me?
¹³ I will bring a drink offering to the Lord,
   to thank him for saving me.
¹⁴ In the meeting of all his people,
   I will give him what I have promised.

¹⁵ How painful it is to the Lord,
  when one of his people dies!
¹⁶ I am your servant, Lord;
  I serve you, just as my mother did.
  You have set me free.
¹⁷ I will give you a sacrifice of thanksgiving,
  and offer my prayer to you.
¹⁸⁻¹⁹ In the meeting of all your people,
  in the courts of your temple, in Jerusalem,
  I will give you what I have promised.

Praise the Lord!

In Praise of the Lord

117 Praise the Lord, all nations!
  Praise him, all peoples!
² His constant love for us is strong,
  and his faithfulness is eternal.

Praise the Lord!

A Prayer of Thanks for Victory

118 Give thanks to the Lord, because
  he is good,
  and his love is eternal.
² Let the people of Israel say,
  "His love is eternal."
³ Let the priests of God say,
  "His love is eternal."
⁴ Let all who fear him say,
  "His love is eternal."

⁵ In my distress I called to the Lord;
  he answered me, and set me free.
⁶ The Lord is with me, I will not be afraid;
  what can men do to me?
⁷ It is the Lord who helps me,
  and I will see my enemies defeated.
⁸ It is better to trust in the Lord,

than to depend on men.
⁹ It is better to trust in the Lord,
  than to depend on human leaders.

¹⁰ Many enemies were round me;
   but I destroyed them by the power of
   the Lord!
¹¹ They were round me on every side;
   but I destroyed them by the power of
   the Lord!
¹² They swarmed round me like bees,
   but they burned out as quickly as a
   brush fire;
   by the power of the Lord I destroyed
   them!
¹³ I was fiercely attacked and was being defeated,
   but the Lord helped me.
¹⁴ The Lord makes me powerful and strong;
   he is my Saviour!

¹⁵ Listen to the glad shouts of victory in the
   tents of God's people:
   "The Lord's mighty power has done it!
¹⁶   His power has brought us victory,
   his mighty power in battle!"

¹⁷ I will not die, but I will live,
   and tell what the Lord has done.
¹⁸ He has punished me severely,
   but he has not let me die.

¹⁹ Open the gates of the temple for me;
   I will go in and praise the Lord!

²⁰ This is the gate of the Lord;
   only the righteous can come in!

²¹ I praise you, Lord, because you heard me,
   because you have given me victory!

²² The stone which the builders rejected as
       worthless,
       turned out to be the most important of
          all.
²³ This was done by the Lord;
       what a wonderful sight it is!
²⁴ What a wonderful day the Lord has given
       us;
       let us be happy, let us celebrate!
²⁵ Save us, Lord, save us!
       Give us success, Lord!

We bless you!

²⁶ God bless him who comes in the name of
       the Lord!
       From the temple of the Lord we bless
          you!
²⁷ The Lord is God; he has been good to us.
       With branches in your hands start the
          festival
       and march round the altar.

²⁸ You are my God, and I give you thanks;
       I will proclaim your greatness.

²⁹ Give thanks to the Lord, because he is
good,
and his love is eternal.

The Law of the Lord

119 Happy are those whose lives are
faultless,
who live according to the law of the
Lord.
² Happy are those who follow his commands,
who obey him with all their heart.
³ Surely they do no wrong;
they walk in the Lord's ways.
⁴ You have given us your laws,
and told us to obey them faithfully.
⁵ How I hope that I shall be faithful
in keeping your rules!
⁶ If I pay attention to all your commandments,
then I will not be disappointed.
⁷ As I learn your righteous rulings,
I will praise you with a pure heart.
⁸ I will obey your laws;
don't ever abandon me!

Obedience to the Law of the Lord

⁹ How can a young man keep his life pure?
By obeying*f* your commands.
¹⁰ With all my heart I try to serve you;
keep me from disobeying your commandments!
¹¹ I keep your law in my heart,
so that I will not sin against you.
¹² I praise you, Lord:
teach me your rules!
¹³ I will repeat aloud
all the laws you have given.

---

fSome ancient translations pure? By obeying; *Hebrew* pure in order
to obey.

¹⁴ I delight in following your commands,
    more than in having great wealth.
¹⁵ I study your instructions;
    I examine your teachings.
¹⁶ I take pleasure in your laws,
    I will not forget your commands.

Happiness in the Law of the Lord

¹⁷ Be good to me, your servant,
    so that I may live and obey your teachings.
¹⁸ Open my eyes, so that I may see
    the wonderful truths in your law.
¹⁹ I am here on earth for just a little while;
    do not hide your commandments from
    me!
²⁰ My heart aches with longing;
    at all times I want to know your judgements.
²¹ You reprimand the proud;
    cursed are those who depart from your
    commands.
²² Free me from their insults and scorn,
    because I have kept your laws.
²³ Even though the rulers meet and plot
    against me,
    I, your servant, will study your rules.
²⁴ Your instructions give me pleasure;
    they are my advisers.

Determination to Obey the Law of the Lord

²⁵ I lie defeated in the dust;
    revive me, as you have promised!
²⁶ I confessed all I have done, and you answered me;
    teach me your rules!
²⁷ Teach me how to obey your laws,
    and I will study your wonderful teachings.
²⁸ I am overcome by sorrow;
    strengthen me, as you have promised.

²⁹ Keep me from going the wrong way,
> and in your goodness teach me your
> law.
³⁰ I have decided to be obedient;
> I have paid attention to your rules.
³¹ I have followed your instructions, Lord;
> don't let me be disappointed!
³² I will eagerly obey your commands,
> because you will give me more under-
> standing.

A Prayer for Understanding

³³ Teach me, Lord, the meaning of your
> laws,
> and I will obey them at all times.
³⁴ Explain your law to me, and I will obey it;
> I will keep it with all my heart.
³⁵ Lead me in the way of your command-
> ments,
> because in them I find happiness.
³⁶ Make me want to obey your rules,
> rather than to get rich.
³⁷ Keep me from paying attention to what is
> worthless;
> be good to me, as you have promised.
³⁸ Keep your promise to me, your servant,
> which you make to those who fear you.
³⁹ Save me from the insults which I fear;
> how wonderful your rules are!
⁴⁰ I want to obey your commands;
> because you are righteous, be good to
> me!

Trusting the Law of the Lord

⁴¹ Show me how much you love me, Lord,
> and save me according to your promise.
⁴² Then I can answer those who insult me,
> because I trust in your word.
⁴³ Enable me to speak the true message at all
> times,
> because my hope is in your judgements.

⁴⁴ I will always obey your law,
forever and ever!
⁴⁵ I will live in complete freedom,
because I have tried to obey your rules.
⁴⁶ I will announce your commands to kings,
and I will not be ashamed.
⁴⁷ I find pleasure in obeying your command-
ments,
because I love them.
⁴⁸ I respect and love your commandments;
I will meditate on your instructions.

Confidence in the Law of the Lord

⁴⁹ Remember your promise to me, your ser-
vant;
it has given me hope.
⁵⁰ Even in my suffering I was comforted,
because your promise gave me life.
⁵¹ The proud have been scornful of me,
but I have not departed from your law.
⁵² I remember the instructions you gave me
in the past,
and they bring me comfort, Lord.
⁵³ I am filled with anger,
when I see the wicked breaking your
law.
⁵⁴ Living far from my real home,
I compose songs about your commands.
⁵⁵ In the night I think of you, Lord,
and I obey your law.
⁵⁶ This is my happiness:
I obey your commands.

Devotion to the Law of the Lord

⁵⁷ You are all I want, Lord;
I promise to obey your laws.
⁵⁸ I ask you with all my heart:
have mercy on me, as you have
promised!
⁵⁹ I have considered my conduct,
and promise to follow your rules.

⁶⁰ Without delay, I hurry
to obey your commandments.
⁶¹ The wicked draw their ropes tight round
me,
but I do not forget your law.
⁶² In the middle of the night I wake up
to praise you for your righteous judgements.
⁶³ I am a friend of all who serve you,
of all who obey your laws.
⁶⁴ Lord, the earth is full of your constant
love;
teach me your commandments!

The Value of the Law of the Lord

⁶⁵ You have kept your promise, Lord,
and you are good to me, your servant.
⁶⁶ Give me wisdom and knowledge,
because I trust in your commands.
⁶⁷ Before you punished me I used to go
wrong,
but now I obey your word.
⁶⁸ How good you are, how kind;
teach me your commands!
⁶⁹ Proud men have told lies about me,
but with all my heart I obey your rules.
⁷⁰ These men have no understanding,
but I find pleasure in your law.
⁷¹ My punishment was good for me,
because it made me learn your commands.
⁷² The law that you give means more to me
than all the money in the world.

The Justice of the Law of the Lord

⁷³ You created me, and you keep me safe;
give me understanding, so that I may
learn your laws.

⁷⁴ Those who fear you will be glad when
    they see me,
        because I trust in your promise.
⁷⁵ I know that your rules are righteous, Lord,
        and that you punished me because you
        are faithful.
⁷⁶ Let your constant love comfort me,
        as you have promised me, your servant.
⁷⁷ Have mercy on me, and I will live,
        because I take pleasure in your law.
⁷⁸ May the proud be ashamed for falsely ac-
    cusing me;
        as for me, I will meditate on your rules.
⁷⁹ May those who fear you come to me,
        and those who know your commands..
⁸⁰ May I perfectly .obey your command-
    ments,
        and be spared the shame of defeat.

Prayer for Deliverance

⁸¹ I am worn out, Lord, waiting for you to
    save me;
        I place my trust in your word.
⁸² My eyes are tired from watching for what
        you promised,
        while I ask, "When will you help me?"
⁸³ I am as useless as a discarded wineskin;
        yet I have not forgot your commands.
⁸⁴ How much longer do I have to wait?
        When will you punish those who perse-
        cute me?
⁸⁵ Proud men, who do not obey your law,
        have dug pits to catch me.
⁸⁶ Your commandments are all trustworthy;
        men persecute me with lies; help me!
⁸⁷ They have almost succeeded in killing me,
        but I have not neglected your rules.
⁸⁸ Because of your constant love, be good to
    me,
        so that I may obey your laws.

Faith in the Law of the Lord

[89] Your word, Lord, will last forever;
it is firm in heaven.

[90] Your faithfulness endures through all the ages;
you have set the earth in place and it remains.

[91] All things remain to this day because of your command,
because they are all your servants.

[92] If your law had not been the source of my joy,
I would have died from my punishment.

[93] I will never neglect your rules,
because by them you have kept me alive.

[94] I am yours—save me!
I have tried to obey your commands.

[95] Wicked men are waiting to kill me,
but I will meditate on your laws.

[96] I have learned that nothing is perfect;
but your commandment has no limits.

Love for the Law of the Lord

[97] How I love your law!
I think about it all day long.

[98] Your commandment is with me all the time,
and makes me wiser than all my enemies.

[99] I understand more than all my teachers,
because I think on your instructions.

[100] I have greater wisdom than old men,
because I obey your commands.

[101] I have avoided all evil conduct,
because I want to obey your word.

[102] I have not neglected your instructions,
because it was you who taught me.

[103] How sweet is the taste of your rules;
they are sweeter than honey!

[104] I gain wisdom from your laws,
and so I hate all bad conduct.

A light for my path

Light from the Law of the Lord

¹⁰⁵ Your word is a lamp to guide me,
and a light for my path.
¹⁰⁶ I will keep my solemn promise
to obey your righteous instructions.
¹⁰⁷ My sufferings, Lord, are terrible indeed;
keep me alive, as you have promised!
¹⁰⁸ Accept my prayer of thanks, Lord,
and teach me your commands.
¹⁰⁹ I am always ready to risk my life;
I have not forgot your law.
¹¹⁰ Wicked men lay a trap for me,
but I have not disobeyed your commands.
¹¹¹ Your commandments are my eternal possession;
they are the joy of my heart.
¹¹² I have decided to obey your rules,
until the day I die.

Safety in the Law of the Lord

¹¹³ I hate those who are not loyal to you,
    but I love your law.
¹¹⁴ You are my defender and protector;
    I hope in your promise.
¹¹⁵ Go away from me, you sinful people!
    I will obey the commandments of my
        God.
¹¹⁶ Give me strength, as you promised, and I
        shall live;
    don't let me be disappointed in my
        hope!
¹¹⁷ Hold me, and I will be safe,
    and I will always pay attention to your
        commands.
¹¹⁸ You reject all who disobey your laws;
    their deceitful schemes are useless.
¹¹⁹ You treat all the wicked like rubbish,
    and so I love your instructions.
¹²⁰ Because of you, I am afraid;
    I am filled with fear because of your
        judgements.

Obedience to the Law of the Lord

¹²¹ I have done what is right and good;
    don't abandon me to my enemies!
¹²² Promise that you will help your servant;
    don't let proud men trouble me!
¹²³ My eyes are tired from watching for your
        salvation,
    for the deliverance you promised.
¹²⁴ Treat me according to your constant love,
    and teach me your commands.
¹²⁵ I am your servant, so give me understand-
        ing
    that I may know your teachings.
¹²⁶ Lord, it is time for you to act,
    because people are disobeying your
        law!
¹²⁷ I love your commands more than gold,
    more than the finest gold.

¹²⁸ And so I follows all your instructions;
    I hate all wrong ways.

Desire to Obey the Law of the Lord

¹²⁹ Your teachings are wonderful;
    I obey them with all my heart.
¹³⁰ The explanation of your teachings gives
    light,
    and brings wisdom to the inexperi-
    enced.
¹³¹ With open mouth I pant,
    in my desire for your commands.
¹³² Turn to me and have mercy on me
    as you do on those who love you.
¹³³ Keep me from falling, as you have prom-
    ised;
    don't let me be overcome by evil.
¹³⁴ Save me from those who oppress me,
    so that I may obey your commands.
¹³⁵ Bless me with your presence,
    and teach me your laws.
¹³⁶ My tears pour down like a river,
    because people do not obey your law.

The Justice of the Law of the Lord

¹³⁷ You are righteous, Lord,
    and your laws are right.
¹³⁸ The rules that you have given
    are completely fair and right.
¹³⁹ My anger burns in me like a fire,
    because my enemies disregard your
    commands.
¹⁴⁰ How certain your promise is!
    How much your servant loves it!
¹⁴¹ I am unimportant and despised,
    but I do not neglect your rules.
¹⁴² Your righteousness will last forever,
    and your law is always true.
¹⁴³ I am filled with trouble and distress,

ᵍ*Some ancient translations* I follow; *Hebrew uncertain.*

but your commandments bring me joy.
¹⁴⁴ Your instructions are righteous forever;
     give me understanding, and I shall live.

Prayer for Deliverance
¹⁴⁵ With all my heart I call to you;
     answer me, Lord, and I will obey your
       commands!
¹⁴⁶ I call to you;
     save me, and I will follow your rules!
¹⁴⁷ Before sunrise I call to you for help;
     I place my hope in your promise.
¹⁴⁸ All night long I lie awake,
     to meditate on your instructions.
¹⁴⁹ Hear me, Lord, according to your con-
       stant love;
     preserve my life, according to your
       goodness!
¹⁵⁰ My cruel persecutors are coming closer,
     people who never keep your law.
¹⁵¹ But you are near to me, Lord,
     and all your promises are true.
¹⁵² Long ago I learned about your instruc-
       tions;
     you made them to last forever.

Plea for Salvation
¹⁵³ Look at my suffering, and save me,
     because I have not neglected your law.
¹⁵⁴ Defend my cause, and set me free;
     save me, as you have promised!
¹⁵⁵ The wicked will not be saved,
     because they do not obey your laws;
¹⁵⁶ but your compassion, Lord, is great,
     so save me, according to your decision.
¹⁵⁷ I have many enemies and oppressors,
     but I do not fail to obey your laws.
¹⁵⁸ When I look at those traitors, I am filled
       with disgust,
     because they do not obey your com-
       mand.

159 See how I love your instructions, Lord!
    Save me, according to your constant
    love.
160 The heart of your law is truth,
    and all your righteous rules are eternal.

Dedication to the Law of the Lord

161 Powerful men attack me unjustly,
    but it is your law that I respect.
162 How happy I am because of your prom-
    ises,
    as happy as someone who finds rich
    treasure.
163 I hate and detest all lies,
    but I love your law.
164 Seven times each day I thank you
    for your righteous judgements.
165 Those who love your law have complete
    security,
    and there is nothing that can make
    them fall.
166 I wait for you to save me, Lord,
    and I do what you command.
167 I obey your rules;
    I love them with all my heart.
168 I obey your commands and your instruc-
    tions;
    you see everything I do.

A Prayer for Help

169 Let my cry for help reach you, Lord!
    Give me understanding, as you have
    promised.
170 Let my prayer come before you,
    and save me, according to your prom-
    ise!
171 I will always praise you,
    because you teach me your rules.
172 I will sing about your law,
    because your commands are just.
173 Be always ready to help me,

because I follow your commands.
¹⁷⁴ How I long for your salvation, Lord!
I find happiness in your law.
¹⁷⁵ Give me life, so that I may praise you;
may your instructions help me!
¹⁷⁶ I wander about like a lost sheep;
so come and look for me, your servant,
because I have not neglected your laws.

A Prayer for Help

120 When I was in trouble I called to
the Lord,
and he answered me.
² Save me, Lord,
from liars and deceivers!

³ You liars, what will God do to you?
How will he punish you?
⁴ With a soldier's sharp arrows,
with red-hot charcoals!

⁵ Living among you is as bad as living in
Meshech,
or among the people of Kedar!
⁶ I have lived too long
with people who hate peace!
⁷ When I speak of peace,
they are for war.

The Lord Our Protector

121 I look to the mountains;
where will my help come from?
² My help comes from the Lord,
who made heaven and earth.

³ May he not let me fall;
may my protector keep awake!

⁴ The protector of Israel
  does not doze or sleep!
⁵ The Lord will guard you;
  he is by your side to protect you.
⁶ The sun will not hurt you during the day,
  nor the moon during the night.

⁷ The Lord will protect you from all danger;
  he will keep you safe.
⁸ He will protect you as you come and go,
  from now on and forever.

In Praise of Jerusalem

122 I was glad when they said to me,
  "Let us go to the Lord's house!"
² And now we are here,
  standing inside the gates of Jerusalem!

³ Jerusalem is a city restored
  in beautiful order and harmony!
⁴ This is where the tribes come,
  the tribes of Israel,
to give thanks to the Lord,
  as he commanded them.
⁵ This is where the law courts are,
  where the king judges his people.

⁶ Pray for the peace of Jerusalem!
  "May those who love you prosper!
⁷   May there be peace inside your walls,
  and safety in your palaces."
⁸ For the sake of my friends and compan-
    ions,
  I say to Jerusalem, "Peace be with
    you!"
⁹ For the sake of the house of the Lord, our
    God,
  I pray for your prosperity.

A Prayer for Mercy

123 Lord, I look up to you,
          up to heaven, where you rule.
2 As the servant depends on his master,
     and the maid depends on her mistress,
   so we keep looking to you, Lord our God,
     until you have mercy on us.

3 Be merciful to us, Lord, be merciful;
     we have been treated with so much con-
       tempt!
4 We have been mocked too long by the
     rich,
     and scorned by proud oppressors!

God the Saviour of His People

124 What if the Lord had not been on
          our side?
        Answer, Israel!
2 "If the Lord had not been on our side,
     when our enemies attacked us,
3 then they would have swallowed us alive,
     in their furious anger against us;
4 then the flood would have carried us
     away,
     the water would have drowned us,
5   the raging torrent would have drowned
       us."

6 Let us thank the Lord,
     who has not let our enemies destroy us.
7 We have escaped like a bird from the hun-
       ter's trap;
     the trap has been broken, and we are
       free!
8 Our help comes from the Lord,
     who made heaven and earth.

The Security of God's People

125 Those who trust in the Lord are
like Mount Zion,
which can never be shaken, never be
moved.
2 As the mountains surround Jerusalem,
so the Lord surrounds his people,
from now on and forever.

3 The wicked will not always rule over the
land of God's people;
if they did, God's people themselves
might do evil.
4 Lord, do good to those who are good,
to those who obey your commands!
5 But punish those who follow their own
wicked ways,
when you punish the evildoers!

Peace be with Israel!

A Prayer for Deliverance

126 When the Lord brought us back
to Zion,
it was like a dream!
2 How we laughed, how we sang for joy!
Then the other nations said about us,
"The Lord did great things for them!"
3 Indeed he did great things for us;
how happy we were!

4 Lord, take us back to our land,
just as your rain brings water back to
dry riverbeds.
5 Let those who cried while they planted,
gather the harvest with joy!

6 Those who cried as they went out carrying
the seed
will come back singing for joy,
bringing in the harvest!

Gather the harvest with joy!

In Praise of God's Goodness

127 If the Lord does not build the house,
the work of the builders is useless;
if the Lord does not protect the city,
it does no good for the sentries to stand guard.
2 It is useless to work so hard for a living,
getting up early and going to bed late,
because the Lord gives rest to those he loves.

3 Children are a gift from the Lord;
they are a real blessing.
4 The sons a man has when he is young
are like arrows in a soldier's hand.
5 Happy is the man who has many such arrows!
He will never be defeated

when he meets his enemies in the place
of judgement.

The Reward of Obedience to the Lord

128 Happy are those who fear the
Lord,
who live by his commands!
2 You will earn enough to provide for your
needs;
you will be happy and prosperous.
3 Your wife will be like a fruitful vine in
your home,
and your sons will be like young olive
trees round your table.
4 A man who obeys the Lord
will surely be blessed like this.

5 May the Lord bless you from Zion!
May you see Jerusalem prosper
all the days of your life!
6 May you live to see your grandchildren!

Peace be with Israel!

Prayer against Israel's Enemies

129 Israel, tell how cruelly your enemies have persecuted you
ever since you were young!
2 "Ever since I was young,
my enemies have persecuted me cruelly,
but they have not overcome me.
3 They cut deep wounds in my back,
and made it like a ploughed field.
4 But the Lord, the righteous one,
has freed me from slavery."

5 May all who hate Zion
be defeated and driven back!
6 May they be like grass growing on the
housetops,

that dries up before it can be cut.
⁷ No one gathers it up,
   or carries it away in bundles.
⁸ No one who passes by will say,
   "May the Lord bless you!
   We bless you in the name of the Lord!"

A Prayer for Help

130 In my despair I call to you, Lord,
² Hear my cry, Lord,
   listen to my call for help!
³ If you kept a record of our sins,
   who could escape being condemned?
⁴ But you forgive us,
   so that we should fear you.

⁵ I wait eagerly for the Lord's help,
   and in his word I trust.
⁶ I wait for the Lord,
   more eagerly than watchmen wait for
      the dawn,
   than watchmen wait for the dawn.

⁷ Israel, trust in the Lord,
   because his love is constant,
   and he is always willing to save.
⁸ He will save his people Israel
   from all their sins.

A Prayer of Humble Trust

131 Lord, I have given up my pride,
      and turned from my arrogance.
I am not concerned with great matters,
   or with subjects too difficult for me.
² But I am content and at peace.
As a child lies quietly in its mother's arms,
   so my heart is quiet within me.
³ Israel, trust in the Lord,
   from now on and forever!

In Praise of the Sanctuary

132 Lord, do not forget David
and all the work he did.
² Remember, Lord, what he promised,
the vow he made to you, the Mighty
God of Israel:
³ "I will not go home or go to bed;
⁴ I will not rest or sleep,
⁵ until I provide a place for the Lord,
a home for the Mighty God of Israel."

⁶ We heard about the covenant box in Bethlehem,
and found it in the fields of Jaar.
⁷ We said, "Let us go to the Lord's house;
let us worship before his throne!"

⁸ Come to your resting place, Lord, with
the covenant box,
the symbol of your power.
⁹ May the priests proclaim that you save
your people;
may all your people shout for joy!

¹⁰ You made a promise to your servant David,
do not reject your chosen king, Lord!
¹¹ You made a solemn promise to David,
and you will not take it back:
"I will make one of your sons king,
and he will rule after you.
¹² If your sons are true to my covenant,
and to the commands I give them,
their sons, also, will follow you as kings
for all time."

¹³ The Lord has chosen Zion;
he wants to make his home there:
¹⁴ "This is where I will live forever;
this is where I want to rule.
¹⁵ I will richly provide Zion with all she
needs;

I will satisfy her poor with food.
¹⁶ I will have her priests proclaim that I save,
and her people will sing and shout for
joy.
¹⁷ Here I will make one of David's descend-
ants a great king;
here I will preserve the rule of my
chosen king.
¹⁸ I will cover his enemies with shame,
but his kingdom will prosper and flourish."

In Praise of Brotherly Love

133 How wonderful it is, how pleasant,
for God's people to live together
like brothers!
² It is like the precious olive oil
running down from Aaron's head and
beard,
down to the collar of his robes.
³ It is like the dew on Mount Hermon,
falling on the hills of Zion.
That is where the Lord has promised his
blessing,
life that never ends.

A Call to Praise God

134 Come, praise the Lord,
all his servants,
all who serve in his temple at night.
² Raise your hands in prayer in the temple,
and praise the Lord!

³ May the Lord, who made heaven and
earth,
bless you from Zion.

A Hymn of Praise

135 Praise the Lord!

Praise his name, you servants of the Lord,
2   who stand in the Lord's house,
    in the sanctuary of our God.
3 Praise the Lord, because he is good;
    sing praises to his name, because he is
     kind.
4 He chose Jacob for himself,
    the people of Israel for his own.

5 I know that our Lord is great;
    he is greater than all the gods.
6 He does whatever he wishes
    in heaven and on earth,
    in the seas and in the depths below.
7 He brings storm clouds from the ends of
     the earth;
    he makes lightning for the storms,
    and brings out the wind from his store-
     room.

8 In Egypt he killed all the firstborn
    of both men and animals.
9 There he performed miracles and wonders
    to punish Pharaoh and all his officials.
10 He destroyed many nations,
    and killed powerful kings:
11 Sihon, king of the Amorites,
    Og, king of Bashan,
    and all the kings in Canaan.
12 He gave their land to his people;
    he gave it to Israel.

13 Lord, men will always know that you are
     God;
    all generations will remember you.
14 The Lord will take pity on his people;
    he will set his servants free.

¹⁵ The idols of the nations are made of silver
and gold;
they are formed by human hands.
¹⁶ They have mouths, but cannot speak,
and eyes, but cannot see.
¹⁷ They have ears, but cannot hear;
there is no breath in their mouths.
¹⁸ May those who made them and all who
trust in them
become like the idols they have made!

¹⁹ Praise the Lord, people of Israel;
praise him, you priests of God!
²⁰ Praise the Lord, you Levites;
praise him, all you that fear him!
²¹ Praise the Lord in Zion,
in Jerusalem, his home.

Praise the Lord!

A Hymn of Thanksgiving

136 Give thanks to the Lord, because
he is good,
and his love is eternal.
² Give thanks to the greatest of all gods;
his love is eternal.
³ Give thanks to the mightiest of all lords;
his love is eternal.

⁴ He alone does great miracles;
his love is eternal.
⁵ By his wisdom he made the heavens;
his love is eternal;
⁶ he built the earth on the deep waters;
his love is eternal.
⁷ He made the sun and the moon;
his love is eternal;
⁸ the sun to rule over the day;
his love is eternal;
⁹ the moon and the stars to rule over the
night;

his love is eternal.
10 He killed the firstborn sons of the
Egyptians;
his love is eternal.
11 He led the people of Israel out of Egypt;
his love is eternal;
12 with his strong hand, his powerful arm;
his love is eternal.
13 He divided the Sea of Reeds;
his love is eternal;
14 he led his people through it;
his love is eternal;
15 he drowned Pharaoh and his army;
his love is eternal.

16 He led his people in the desert;
his love is eternal.
17 He killed powerful kings;
his love is eternal;
18 he killed famous kings;
his love is eternal;
19 Sihon, king of the Amorites;
his love is eternal;
20 and Og, king of Bashan;
his love is eternal.
21 He gave their land to his people;
his love is eternal;
22 he gave it to Israel, his servant;
his love is eternal.

23 He did not forget us when we were defeated;
his love is eternal;
24 he freed us from our enemies;
his love is eternal.
25 He gives food to all men and animals;
his love is eternal.

26 Give thanks to the God of heaven;
his love is eternal.

The Lament of Israelites in Exile

137 By the rivers of Babylon
      we sat and cried when we
         remembered Zion.
2 On the willows nearby
   we hung our harps.
3 Those who captured us told us to sing;
   they told us to entertain them:
   "Sing us a song about Zion!"

4 How can we sing the Lord's song
   in a foreign land?
5 May I never be able to play the harp again,
   if I forget you, Jerusalem!
6 May I never be able to sing again,
   if I do not remember you,
   if I do not think of you as my greatest
      joy!

7 Remember, Lord, what the Edomites did,
   the day Jerusalem was captured.
Remember how they kept saying,
   "Tear it down to the ground!"
8 Babylon, you will be destroyed!
Happy is the man who pays you back
   for what you have done to us—
9   who takes your babies,
   and smashes them on a rock!

A Prayer of Thanksgiving

138 I thank you, Lord, with all my
      heart:
   I sing praise to you before the gods.
2 I bow down in front of your holy temple
   and praise your name,
because of your constant love and faith-
      fulness,
   because you have shown that you and
      your commands are supreme.*h*

*h*shown that you and your commands are supreme; *Hebrew* shown
that your command is greater than all your name.

³ You answered me when I called to you;
 with your strength you strengthened
 me.

⁴ All the kings of the earth will praise you,
 Lord,
 because they have heard your promises.
⁵ They will sing about what the Lord has
 done,
 and about his great glory.
⁶ Even though the Lord is so high above,
 he cares for the lowly,
 and the proud cannot hide from him.

⁷ Even when I am surrounded by troubles,
 you keep me safe;
 you oppose my angry enemies,
 and save me by your power.
⁸ You will do everything you have promised me;
 Lord, your love is constant forever.
 Complete the work that you have
 begun.

God's Complete Knowledge and Care

139 Lord, you have examined me, and
 you know me.
² You know everything I do;
 from far away you understand all my
 thoughts.
³ You see me, whether I am working or
 resting;
 you know all my actions.
⁴ Even before I speak
 you already know what I will say.
⁵ You are all round me, on every side;
 you protect me with your power.
⁶ Your knowledge of me is overwhelming;
 it is too deep for me to understand.

⁷ Where could I go to escape from your
        spirit?
    Where could I get away from your pres-
        ence?
⁸ If I went up to heaven, you would be
        there;
    if I lay down in the world of the dead,
        you would be there.
⁹ If I flew away beyond the east,
    or lived in the farthest place in the west,
¹⁰ you would be there to lead me,
    you would be there to help me.
¹¹ I could ask the darkness to hide me,
    or the light round me to turn into night,
¹² but even the darkness is not dark for you,
    and the night is as bright as the day.
    Darkness and light are the same to you.

¹³ You created every part of me;
    you put me together in my mother's
        womb.
¹⁴ I praise you because you are to be feared;
    all you do is strange and wonderful.
    I know it with all my heart.
¹⁵ You saw my bones being formed,
    carefully put together in my mother's
        womb,
    when I was growing there in secret.
¹⁶ You saw me before I was born.
    The days that had been created for me
    had all been recorded in your book,
    before any of them had ever begun.
¹⁷ God, how difficult your thoughts are for
        me;
    how many of them there are!
¹⁸ If I counted them, they would be more
        than the grains of sand.
    When I awake, I am still with you.

¹⁹ God, how I wish you would kill the
        wicked!

How I wish violent men would leave me
   alone!
20 They say wicked things about you;
   they speak evil things against your
   name.[i]
21 Lord, how I hate those who hate you!
   How I despise those who rebel against
   you!
22 My hatred for them is complete;
   I regard them as my enemies.

23 Examine me, God, and know my mind;
   test me, and discover my thoughts.
24 Find out if there is any deceit in me,
   and guide me in the eternal way.

A Prayer for Protection

140 Save me, Lord, from evil men;
   keep me safe from violent men.
2 They are always plotting evil,
   always stirring up quarrels.
3 Their tongues are like deadly snakes,
   their words are like a cobra's poison.

4 Protect me, Lord, from the power of the
   wicked;
   keep me safe from violent men,
   who plot my downfall.
5 Proud men have laid a trap for me;
   they have spread a net of ropes,
   and along the path they have set traps
   to catch me.

6 I say to the Lord, "You are my God."
   Hear my cry for help, Lord!
7 Lord, my God, my strong Saviour,
   you have protected me in battle.
8 Lord, don't give the wicked what they
   want;
   don't let their evil plots succeed!

[i]Hebrew unclear.

⁹ Don't let my enemies be victorious;⸍
    make their threats against me fall back
        on them.
¹⁰ May red-hot coals fall on them;
    may they be thrown into a pit and never
        get out.
¹¹ May those who accuse others falsely not
        succeed;
    may evil overtake the violent man and
        destroy him.

¹² I know that you, Lord, defend the cause of
        the poor,
    and the rights of the needy.
¹³ The righteous will praise you indeed;
    they will live in your presence.

An Evening Prayer

141 I call to you, Lord; help me now!
        Listen to me when I call to you.
² Receive my prayer as incense,
    my uplifted hands as an evening sac-
        rifice.

³ Lord, place a guard at my mouth,
    a sentry at the door of my lips.
⁴ Keep me from wanting to do wrong,
    or to join evil men in their wickedness.
May I never take part in their feasts!

⁵ A good man may punish me and repri-
        mand me in kindness,
    but I will not let an evil man anoint my
        head,
    because I am always praying against his
        evil deeds.
⁶ When their rulers are thrown down on
        rocky cliffs,

Don't let my enemies be victorious; *Hebrew unclear.*

the people will admit that my words
    were true.
7 Like wood that is split and chopped into
    bits,
    so their bones are scattered at the edge
      of the grave.*k*

8 But I, Lord God, keep trusting in you;
    I seek your protection;
    don't let me die!
9 Protect me from the traps they have set
    for me,
    from the snares of those evildoers.
10 May the wicked fall into their own traps,
    while I go by unharmed.

A Prayer for Help*l*

142   I call to the Lord for help;
      I plead with him.
2 I bring him all my complaints;
    I tell him all my troubles.
3 When I am ready to give up,
    he knows what I should do.
In the path where I walk.
    my enemies have hidden a trap for me.
4 I look beside me and I see
    that there is no one to help me;
there is no one to protect me;
    no one cares for me.

5 Lord, I cry to you for help;
    you, Lord, are my protector;
    you are all I want in this life.
6 Listen to my cry for help,
    because I am sunk in despair.
Save me from my enemies,
    who are much stronger than I am.
7 Rescue me from my trouble;

*kVerses 5–7 in Hebrew are unclear. lHebrew title: A Prayer of
David when he was in the cave.*

then in the meeting of your people I will
    praise you,
because you have been good to me.

A Prayer for Help

143 Lord, hear my prayer,
    listen to my plea!
You are righteous and faithful,
    so answer me!
2 Don't put me, your servant, on trial;
    no one is innocent in your sight.

3 My enemy has persecuted me,
    and completely defeated me.
He has put me in a dark prison,
    and I am like those who died long ago.
4 So I am ready to give up;
    I am in deep despair.

5 I remember the days gone by;
    I think about all that you have done,
    I bring to mind all your deeds.
6 I lift up my hands to you in prayer;
    like dry ground my soul thirsts for you.

7 Answer me now, Lord!
    I have lost all hope!
Don't hide yourself from me,
    or I will be among those who go down
      to the land of the dead.
8 I trust in you;
    in the morning remind me of your con-
      stant love.
My prayers go up to you;
    show me the way I should go.

9 I go to you for protection, Lord;
    rescue me from my enemies.
10 You are my God;
    teach me to do your will.
May your spirit be good to me
    and guide me on a safe path.

[11] Save me, Lord, as you have promised;
    in your goodness, rescue me from my
        troubles!
[12] In your love for me, kill my enemies,
    and destroy all my oppressors,
    because I am your servant.

A King Thanks God for Victory

144 Praise the Lord, my protector;
    he trains me for battle,
and prepares me for war.
[2] He is my protector[m] and defender,
    my shelter and Saviour,
    in whom I trust for safety.
He subdues the nations under me.

[3] Lord, what is man, that you notice him;
    mere man, that you pay attention to
        him?
[4] He is like a puff of wind;
    his days are like a passing shadow.

[5] Lord, pull back the sky, and come down;
    touch the mountains, and they will pour
        out smoke.
[6] Send flashes of lightning, and scatter your
        enemies;
    shoot your arrows, and send them run-
        ning!
[7] Reach down from above,
    pull me out of the deep water, and save
        me;
    save me from the power of foreigners,
[8] who never tell the truth,
    and lie even under oath.

[9] I will sing you a new song, God;
    I will play the harp and sing to you.

---

[m]protector *(as in Ps. 18.2 and 2 Sam. 22.2); Hebrew* love.

¹⁰ You give victory to kings,
    and rescue your servant David.
¹¹ Save me from my cruel enemies,
    rescue me from the power of foreigners,
who never tell the truth,
    and lie even under oath.

¹² May our sons in their youth
    be like plants that grow up strong.
May our daughters be like statues,
    which adorn the corners of a palace.
¹³ May our barns be filled
    with crops of every kind.
May the sheep in our fields
    bear young by the tens of thousands.
¹⁴ May our cattle reproduce plentifully,
    without miscarriage or loss.
May there be no cries of distress in our
    streets!

¹⁵ Happy is the nation of whom this is true;
    happy are the people whose God is the
    Lord!

A Hymn of Praise

145 I will proclaim your greatness, my
    God and king;
I will thank you forever and ever.
² Every day I will thank you;
    I will praise you forever and ever.
³ The Lord is great, and must be highly
    praised;
his greatness is beyond understanding.

⁴ What you have done will be praised from
    one generation to the next;
they will proclaim your mighty acts.
⁵ Men will speak of your glory and majesty,
    and I will meditate on your wonderful
    deeds.

⁶ Men will speak of your mighty acts,
and I will proclaim your greatness.
⁷ They will tell about all your goodness,
and sing about your kindness.

⁸ The Lord is loving and merciful,
slow to become angry and full of constant love.
⁹ He is good to everyone
and has compassion on all he made.

¹⁰ All your creatures, Lord, will praise you,
and your people will give you thanks!
¹¹ They will speak of the glory of your kingdom,
and tell of your might,
¹² so that all men will know your mighty
acts,
and the glorious majesty of your kingdom.
¹³ Your kingdom is eternal,
and you are king forever.

The Lord is faithful to his promises,
and good in all he does.
¹⁴ He helps all who are in trouble;
he raises all who are humbled.
¹⁵ All living things look hopefully to him,
and he gives them food when they need
it.
¹⁶ He gives them enough
and satisfies the needs of all.
¹⁷ The Lord is righteous in all he does,
merciful in all his acts.
¹⁸ He is near to all who call to him,
who call to him with sincerity.
¹⁹ He supplies the needs of all who fear him;
he hears their cry and saves them.
²⁰ He protects all who love him,
but he will destroy all the wicked.

²¹ I will always praise the Lord;
    let all creatures praise his holy name
      forever!

In Praise of God the Saviour

146 Praise the Lord!
      Praise the Lord, my soul!
² I will praise him as long as I live;
    I will sing to my God all my life.

³ Don't put your trust in human leaders,
    or anyone else who cannot save you.
⁴ When they die they return to the soil;
    on that day all their plans come to an
      end.

⁵ Happy is the man who has the God of
      Jacob to help him,
    and depends on the Lord his God,
⁶ who created heaven, earth, and sea,
    and all that is in them.
He always keeps his promises;
⁷   he judges in favour of the oppressed
    and gives food to the hungry.

The Lord sets prisoners free
⁸   and gives sight to the blind.
He raises all who are humbled;
    he loves his righteous people.
⁹ He protects the foreigners who live in the
      land;
    he helps widows and orphans,
    but ruins the plans of the wicked.

¹⁰ The Lord will be king forever!
    Your God, Zion, will reign for all time!

Praise the Lord!

And gives food to the hungry

In Praise of God the Almighty

147 Praise the Lord!

It is good to sing praise to our God;
  it is pleasant and right to praise him.
² The Lord is restoring Jerusalem;
  he is bringing back the exiles.
³ He heals the brokenhearted,
  and bandages their wounds.

⁴ He has determined the number of the
    stars
  and calls each one by name.
⁵ Great and almighty is our Lord;
  his knowledge cannot be measured.
⁶ He raises the humble,
  but crushes the wicked to the ground.

7 Sing hymns of praise to the Lord;
    play music to our God on the harp.
8 He spreads clouds over the sky;
    he provides rain for the earth,
    and makes grass grow on the hills.
9 He gives animals their food,
        and feeds the young ravens when they
        call.

10 His pleasure is not in strong horses,
    nor his delight in brave soldiers;
11 but he takes pleasure in those who fear
        him,
    in those who trust in his constant love.

12 Praise the Lord, Jerusalem!
    Praise your God, Zion!
13 He keeps your gates strong;
    he blesses your people.
14 He keeps your borders safe
    and satisfies you with the best wheat.

15 He gives an order,
    and it comes quickly to the earth.
16 He sends snow as thick as wool,
    and scatters frost like dust.
17 He sends hail like gravel;
    no one can endure the cold he sends!
18 Then he gives a command, and melts the
        ice,
    he sends the wind, and the water flows.

19 He gives his message to Jacob,
    his instructions and laws to Israel.
20 He has not done this for other nations;
    they do not know his laws.

Praise the Lord!

A Call for the Universe to Praise God

148 Praise the Lord!

Praise the Lord from heaven,
   you that live in the heights above!
2 Praise him, all his angels,
   all his heavenly armies!

3 Praise him, sun and moon;
   praise him, shining stars!
4 Praise him, highest heavens,
   and the waters above the sky!

5 Let them all praise the name of the Lord!
He commanded, and they were created;
6   by his command they were fixed in their
      places forever,
   and they cannot disobey.

7 Praise the Lord from the earth,
   sea monsters and all ocean depths;
8 lightning and hail, snow and clouds,
   strong winds that obey his command!

9 Praise him, hills and mountains,
   fruit trees and forests;
10 all animals, tame and wild,
   reptiles and birds!

11 Praise him, kings and all peoples,
   princes and all other rulers;
12 young men and girls,
   old people and children also!

13 Let them all praise the name of the Lord.
His name is greater than all others;
   his glory is above earth and heaven!
14 He made his nation strong,

so that all his people praise him,
the people of Israel, so dear to him!

Praise the Lord!

A Hymn of Praise

149 Praise the Lord!

Sing a new song to the Lord;
praise him in the meeting of his faithful
people!
2 Be glad, Israel, because of your creator;
rejoice, people of Zion, because of your
king!
3 Praise his name with dancing;
play drums and harps in praise of him.

4 The Lord takes pleasure in his people;
he honours the humble with victory.
5 Let God's people rejoice in their triumph,
and sing joyfully at their feasts.
6 Let them shout aloud as they praise God,
with their sharp swords in their hands;
7 to defeat the nations,
and to punish the peoples;
8 to tie up their kings in chains,
their leaders in chains of iron;
9 to punish the nations as God has commanded.
This is the victory of God's people!

Praise the Lord!

Praise the Lord!

150 Praise the Lord!

Praise God in his temple!
Praise his strength in heaven!

² Praise him for the mighty things he has
   done!
   Praise his supreme greatness!

³ Praise him with trumpets!
   Praise him with harps and lyres!
⁴ Praise him with drums and dancing!
   Praise him with harps and flutes!
⁵ Praise him with cymbals!
   Praise him with loud cymbals!
⁶ Praise the Lord, all living creatures!

   Praise the Lord!

Praise the Lord!

WORD LIST

WORD LIST

Abyss The place in the depths of the earth where the demons were imprisoned until their final punishment.

Agate A semiprecious stone of various colors, but usually white and brown.

Alabaster A soft stone of usually light creamy color, from which vases and jars were made.

Aloes A sweet-smelling substance, derived from a plant. It was used medicinally and as a perfume.

Amen A Hebrew word which means "it is so" or "may it be so." It can also be translated "certainly," "truly," or "surely." In Revelation 3.14 it is used as a title for Christ.

Amethyst A semiprecious stone, usually purple or violet in color.

Anoint To pour or rub olive oil on someone in order to honor him or to appoint him to some special work. The Israelite kings were anointed as a sign of their taking office, and so the king could be called "the anointed one." In a figurative sense, "The Anointed One" is the title of the one whom God chose and appointed as Savior and Lord.

Apostle Principally one of the group of twelve men whom Jesus chose to be his special followers and helpers. It is also used in the New Testament to refer to Paul and other Christian workers. The word may have the sense of "messenger."

Areopagus A hill in Athens where the city council used to meet. For this reason the council itself was called Areopagus, even after it no longer met on the hill.

Artemis The Greek name of an ancient goddess of fertility, worshiped especially in Asia Minor.

Baal The god of fertility worshiped by the Canaanites; his female counterpart was Asherah. After the Hebrews invaded Canaan, many of them began worshiping these two gods.

Barley A cultivated grain similar to wheat, grown as a food crop.

Beelzebul A New Testament name given to the Devil as the chief of the evil spirits.

Beryl A semiprecious stone, usually green or bluish green in color.

Breastplate Part of a soldier's armor, made of leather or metal; it covered the chest and sometimes the back as a protection against arrows and the blows of a sword.

Carnelian A semiprecious stone, usually red in color.

Chalcedony A semiprecious stone, usually milky or gray in color.

Christ Originally a title, the Greek equivalent of the Hebrew word "Messiah." It means "the anointed one." Jesus was called the Christ because he was the one whom God chose and sent as Savior and Lord.

Circumcise To cut off the foreskin of the penis. As a sign of God's covenant with his people Israelite boys were circumcised eight days after they were born (Genesis 17.9–14).

Council The supreme religious court of the Jews, composed of seventy leaders of the Jewish people and presided over by the High Priest.

Covenant An agreement, either between persons or between God and a person or a people.

Covenant Box The wooden chest covered with gold, in which were kept the two stone tablets on which were written the Ten Commandments. It has traditionally been called the Ark of the Covenant.

Cumin A small plant whose seeds are ground up and used for seasoning foods.

Dedication, Festival of The Jewish festival, lasting eight days, which celebrated the restoration and re-dedication in 165 B.C. of the Temple altar by the Jewish patriot Judas Maccabeus. The festival began on the 25th day of the month Kislev (around December 10). The Jewish name for this festival is Hannukah.

Defile To make ritually unclean or impure. Certain foods and practices were prohibited by the Law of Moses because they were thought to make a person ritually or ceremonially unclean. Such a person could not take part in the public worship until he had performed certain rituals which would remove the defilement.

Demon An evil spirit with the power to harm people; it was regarded as a messenger and servant of the Devil.

Dill A small garden plant whose stems, leaves, and seeds are used for seasoning food.

Disciple A person who follows and learns from someone else. In the New Testament the word is used of the followers of John the Baptist and especially of the followers of Jesus, particularly the twelve apostles.

Dragon A legendary beast, thought to be like a huge lizard. It is also called a serpent and appears as a figure of the Devil (Revelation 12.3—13.4; 20.2-3).

Elders In the Old Testament this is a name given to certain respected leaders of a tribe, nation, or city. In the New Testament three different groups are called elders: (1) in the Gospels the elders are influential Jewish religious leaders, some of whom were members of the supreme Council; (2) in Acts 11-21 and the Letters the elders are Christian church officers who had general responsibility for the work of the church; (3) in Revelation the twenty-four elders are part of God's court in heaven, perhaps as representatives of God's people.

Epicureans Those who followed the teaching of Epicurus (died 270 B.C.), a Greek philosopher who taught that happiness is the highest good in life.

Epileptic A person who suffers from a nervous disease causing convulsions and fainting.

Eunuch A man who has been made physically incapable of having normal sexual relations. Eunuchs were often important officials in the courts of ancient kings, and the term may have come to be used of such officials in general, regardless of their sexual condition.

Fast To go without food for a while as a religious duty.

Frankincense A valuable incense, made from the sap of a certain tree. This incense was probably imported from Arabia.

Gentile A person who is not a Jew.

Hades The Greek name used in the New Testament to refer to the world of the dead.

Harvest Festival The Israelite festival celebrating the wheat harvest, held in the latter part of May, fifty days after Passover. The Jewish name for this festival is Shavuoth (the Feast of Weeks). It has also been called Pentecost.

Hermes The name of a Greek god who served as messenger of the gods.

Herod's party A political party in New Testament times composed of Jews who favored being ruled by one of the descendants of Herod the Great rather than by the Roman governor.

High Priest The priest who occupied the highest office in the Jewish priestly system and was president of the supreme Council of the Jews. Once a year (on the Day of Atonement) he would enter the Most Holy Place in the Temple and offer sacrifice for himself and for the sins of the people of Israel.

Hyssop A small bushy plant, used in religious ceremonies to sprinkle liquids.

Incense Material which is burned in order to produce a pleasant smell. The Israelites used it in their worship.

Jasper A semiprecious stone of various colors. The

jasper mentioned in the Bible was probably green, or else clear.

Law   The name which the Jews applied to the first five books of the Old Testament, also called "The Books of Moses." Sometimes, however, the name is applied in a more general way to the entire Old Testament.

Levite   (1) A member of the tribe of Levi; (2) a man who assisted the priest in the performance of religious duties.

Living creatures (also referred to as "winged creatures" and traditionally called "cherubim")   Symbols of God's majesty and associated with his presence. For a description of such creatures see Exodus 25.18-20; Ezekiel 1.5-13; 10; Revelation 4.6-9.

Manna   A food eaten by the Israelites during their travels in the wilderness. It was white and flaky and looked like small seeds (Exodus 16.14-21; Numbers 11.7-9).

Messiah   A Hebrew title (meaning "the anointed one") given to the promised Savior, whose coming was foretold by the Hebrew prophets; the corresponding Greek term "the Christ" has the same meaning.

Most Holy Place   The innermost room of the Tent of the LORD's presence or the Temple. The Covenant Box was kept there. Only the High Priest could enter the Most Holy Place, and he did so only once a year, on the Day of Atonement.

Mustard   A large plant which grows from a very small seed. The seeds were ground into powder and used as spice on food.

Myrrh   A sweet-smelling resin that was highly prized. It served as a medicine (Mark 15.23) and was used by the Jews in preparing bodies for burial (John 19.39).

Nard   An expensive perfume made from a plant.

Nazarene Someone from the town of Nazareth. The name was used as a title for Jesus and also as a name for the early Christians (Acts 24.5).

New Moon Festival A religious observance held by the Israelites on the day of each new moon.

Onyx A semiprecious stone of various colors.

Outcasts In the Gospels this name, which in many translations appears as "sinners," refers to those Jews who had been excluded from synagogue worship because they violated rules about foods that should not be eaten and about associating with people who were not Jews. Such outcasts were despised by many of their fellow Jews, and Jesus was criticized for associating with them (Mark 2.15–17; Luke 7.34; 15.1–2).

Parable A story which teaches spiritual truth; it was often used by Jesus.

Paradise A name for heaven (Luke 23.43; 2 Corinthians 12.3).

Paralytic Someone who suffers from a disease that prevents him from moving part or all of his body.

Passover The Israelite festival, on the 14th day of the month Nisan (around April 1), which celebrated the deliverance of the ancient Hebrews from their captivity in Egypt. The Angel of Death killed the first-born in the Egyptian homes but passed over the Hebrew homes (Exodus 12.23–27). The Jewish name for this festival is Pesach.

Pentecost, Day of The Greek name for the Israelite festival of wheat harvest (see Harvest Festival). The name Pentecost (meaning "fiftieth") comes from the fact that the feast was held fifty days after Passover.

Pharisees A Jewish religious party during the time of Jesus. They were strict in obeying the Law of Moses and other regulations which had been added to it through the centuries.

Preparation, Day of The sixth day of the week (Friday), on which the Jews made the required preparations to observe the Sabbath (Saturday).

Prophet A person who proclaims a message from God. The term usually refers to certain men in the Old Testament, but the New Testament speaks of prophets in the early church. John the Baptist is also called a prophet.

Quartz A semiprecious stone of various colors, but usually clear.

Rabbi A Hebrew word which means "my teacher."

Red Sea Evidently referred originally to (1) a series of lakes and marshes between the head of the Gulf of Suez and the Mediterranean, the region generally regarded as the site of the events described in Exodus 13, and was also used to designate (2) the Gulf of Suez, (3) the Gulf of Aqaba.

Rephan The name of an ancient god that was worshiped as the ruler of the planet Saturn.

Sabbath The seventh day of the Jewish week (from sundown on Friday to sundown on Saturday), a holy day on which no work was permitted.

Sackcloth A coarse cloth made of goats' hair, which was worn as a sign of mourning or distress.

Sadducees A small Jewish religious party in New Testament times, composed largely of priests. They based their beliefs primarily on the first five books of the Old Testament and differed in several matters of belief and practice from the larger party of the Pharisees.

Samaritan A name used to refer to a native of Samaria, the region between Judea and Galilee. Because of differences in politics, race, customs, and religion (including especially the central place of worship), there was much bad feeling between the Jews and the Samaritans.

Sapphire A very valuable stone, usually blue in color.

Scorpion A small creature which has eight legs and a long tail with a poisonous sting. It can inflict a very painful, and sometimes fatal, wound.

Scriptures In the New Testament the word refers to the collected body of Hebrew sacred writings, known to Christians as the Old Testament. Various names are used: the Law (or the Law of Moses) and the prophets (Matthew 5.17; 7.12; Luke 2.22; 24.44; Acts 13.15; 28.23); the Holy Scriptures (Romans 1.2; 2 Timothy 3.15); the old covenant (2 Corinthians 3.14). The singular "scripture" refers to a single passage of the Old Testament.

Serpent A name given to the dragon, which appears in the New Testament as a figure of the Devil (Revelation 12.3–17; 20.2–3).

Shelters, Festival of A joyous festival celebrated by the Israelites in the fall after the completion of the harvest. In order to help them remember the years when their ancestors wandered through the wilderness, the Israelites constructed rough shelters to live in during the festival. The Jewish name for this festival is Sukkoth. It has been traditionally called the Feast of Tabernacles or the Feast of Booths.

Sickle A tool consisting of a curved metal blade and a wooden handle, used for cutting wheat and other crops.

Stoics Those who followed the teachings of the Greek philosopher Zeno (died 265 B.C.), who taught that happiness is to be found in being free from pleasure and pain.

Sulfur In the Bible this refers to a sulfur compound which burns with great heat and produces an unpleasant smell.

Teachers of the Law Men who in New Testament times taught and interpreted the teachings of the Old Testament, especially the first five books.

Tenant A man who grows crops on land owned by someone else, and turns over a part of the harvest to the owner to pay for the use of his land.

Topaz A semiprecious stone, usually yellow in color.

Turquoise A semiprecious stone, blue or bluish green in color.

Unleavened Bread, Festival of   The Israelite festival, lasting seven days after Passover; it also celebrated the deliverance of the ancient Hebrews from Egypt. The name came from the practice of not using leaven (yeast) in making bread during that week (Exodus 12.14–20). It was held from the 15th to the 22nd day of the month Nisan (around the first week of April).

Vow   A strong declaration or promise, usually made while calling upon God to punish the speaker if the statement should prove to be not true or if the promise were not kept.

Winged creatures (also referred to as "living creatures" and traditionally called "cherubim") Symbols of God's majesty and associated with his presence. For a description of such creatures see Exodus 25.18–20; Ezekiel 1.5–13; 10; Revelation 4.6–9.

Winnowing shovel   A tool like a shovel or a large fork, used to separate the wheat from the chaff.

Wreath   Flowers or leaves arranged in a circle, to be placed on a person's head. In ancient times a wreath of leaves was the prize given to winners in athletic contests.

Yeast   A substance, also called leaven, which is added to dough made from the flour of wheat or barley to make it rise before being baked into bread.

Yoke   A heavy bar of wood fitted over the necks of two oxen to make it possible for them to pull a plow or a cart. The word is used figuratively to describe the moral lessons that a teacher passes on to his pupils.

Zeus   The name of the supreme god of the Greeks.

Zion   Originally a designation for "David's City," the Jebusite stronghold captured by King David's forces. The term "Zion" was later extended in meaning to refer to the hill on which the Temple stood.

SUBJECT INDEX

SUBJECT INDEX

A

Aaron 322, 559, 562, 565
Abel 66, 190, 571, 576
Abraham 6, 205, 262, 389-391, 475-477, 571-572, 584
Achaia 354-355, 357, 413, 449-450, 463, 517
Adam 391-392, 445, 447, 532
Aeneas 329
Agabus 335, 362
Agrippa
   Herod Agrippa I 335-337
   Herod Agrippa II 372-376
Ananias
   of Damascus 328, 366
   High Priest 367, 370
   Ananias and Sapphira 315
Andrew 8, 88, 130, 239-240, 252, 275
Angels
   messengers and agents of God 2-3, 7, 37, 46, 69, 72, 84-85, 147-149, 152-153, 240, 316, 325, 330, 336-337, 377, 525, 553, 624, 658-659
   in heaven 63, 191, 201, 218, 512, 533, 536, 628, 632, 634-640, 644, 646-648, 650-651, 653, 656
   guardian angels 49
   destroying angels 337
   devil and his angels 73, 467, 621, 641-642
   names
      Gabriel 147-149
      Michael 621, 641-642
      Apollyon 637
Anna 154
Annas 156, 289-290, 313
Antioch
   in Syria 319, 334-335, 338, 344, 347, 474
   in Pisidia 339-341, 344
Apollos 355, 421, 423, 449
Apostle 24, 106, 166, 305-307, 622, 656
Aquila 353, 355, 413, 449, 544
Arabia 307, 473, 480
Areopagus 352

Ark *of Noah* see Boat
Artemis 357-358
Ascension 145, 235, 305
Athens,-ians 351, 352, 353
Augustus 151

B

Baal 404
Babylon 599, 644, 648, 650-652
Baptism
   John the Baptist 5-6, 88, 156-157, 238, 244, 340, 355-356
   Jesus 6, 88, 157
   Christian 85, 310, 324-326, 333, 393, 439, 472, 511, 596
   with the Spirit 6, 88, 157, 239, 305, 334
Barabbas 80, 140, 228, 292
Bar-Jesus 338
Barnabas 315, 335, 338, 341-347
Bartholomew 24, 96, 166, 306
Bartimaeus 121
Beatitudes 9-10, 166-167
Beelzebul 26, 31-32, 96, 188 (*see* Devil, Satan)
"Benedictus" 151
Berea 351, 359
Bernice 373, 376
Bethany
   near Jerusalem 59, 74, 132, 270, 273-274
   beyond Jordan 238
Bethlehem 3-4, 152-153
Bethphage 57, 122, 213
Bethsaida 29, 107, 113, 178, 240
Blood
   of animals 565-567, 573
   of men 647, 649, 652
   of Christ 75, 134, 223, 255, 296, 435, 438, 565-566, 570, 576-577, 590, 607, 614, 634, 642, 653
Boat (Ark of Noah) 69, 571, 596
Boaz 2
Bread
   material 6-7, 44-45, 105, 234, 252, 301

figurative 253-255
offered to God 30, 94, 165, 565
Lord's Supper 75, 134, 223, 437
Burial
of Jesus 83, 133, 142-143, 231-232, 274, 296-297
of others 39, 309, 315-316, 324
figurative 393, 511

C

Caesar *see* Emperor
Caesarea
seaport 326, 330-331, 334, 337, 362-363, 369-370, 372
Philippi 45, 113
Caiaphas 73, 77, 156, 273, 289-290, 313
Cain 570, 610, 621
Calvary *see* Golgotha
Cana 240-241, 248, 299
Capernaum 8, 19, 29, 48, 89, 91, 117, 241, 253, 255
Cherubim *see* Winged Creatures
Cenchreae 355, 413
Chief Priests 3, 59, 79-80, 114, 139-140, 179, 216-217, 258, 293-294, 314, 317, 328, 372-373
Church(es) 45, 51, 329, 361, 413-416, 440-444, 486, 494
Church Ministers
general 440, 490
leaders 497, 532, 546
elders 335, 344-346, 360, 534-536, 546, 588, 616, 618
helpers 497, 532-533
Cilicia 319, 346, 347, 365, 473
Circumcise,-cision
literal 150, 153, 257, 320, 344-345, 347, 387, 389-390, 428, 473, 480-481, 483, 502, 511
figurative 502, 511
Cleopas 233
Clopas 295
Coming of Christ, Lord, Son of Man (final) 46, 67-70, 131-132, 194, 207-208, 221-222, 280, 305, 504, 519, 521-522, 525-526, 567, 604-605, 609-610, 658-659
Command,-ments
of Jewish Law 10-13, 53-54, 63-64, 91, 127-128, 259-260, 395-396, 409
of God and Christ 9-18, 276, 279, 282, 611, 616
Conscience 386, 400, 408, 430-431, 436, 546, 566, 596
Corinth 353-355, 416-470
Cornelius 330-334
Cornerstone 488, 593
Covenant
old (with Israel) 312, 320, 455, 476, 487, 564-567
new 75, 134, 223, 438, 454, 563-564, 566, 568, 570, 576, 578
Covenant Box 565, 640
Covetousness 192-193, 395, 492, 512, 586
Create,-tion
universe 237, 509, 563, 570, 638
new nature 491
Crete,-ans 376-377, 546
Cross
of Christ 81-83, 141-142, 229-231, 293-296, 393, 417, 483, 488, 509, 511, 574
of Christ's disciples 26, 46, 114, 179, 200, 393, 475, 483
Crown
literal 81, 140, 292-293
figurative 540, 544, 554-555, 598, 626, 632, 645
Cyprus 315, 338-339, 347
Cyrene 81, 141, 229, 307, 335

D

Damascus 327-329, 365-366, 374-375, 468, 473
Darkness
literal 82, 142, 575
spiritual 8, 226, 237, 244, 275-276, 455-456, 492-493, 607, 608
David 1-2, 64, 128, 152, 219, 306, 309-310, 322, 339-340, 383, 389, 540, 628, 631, 659

Day of Judgment 18, 25, 29, 32, 72–73, 221–222, 254, 276, 386, 521–522, 539, 544, 569, 604–605, 612, 655

Death
physical 445–447, 521
    Ananias and Sapphira 315–316
    Antipas 626
    Christian martyrs 633, 649, 654
    Herod Agrippa I 337–338
    James 335
    John the Baptist 38–39, 105–106
    Lazarus 270–272
    Old Testament prophets 66, 190, 570–574
    Simon Peter 301–302
    Stephen 323–324
figurative 391–396, 581, 589, 611, 614, 654–655
of Christ 82–83, 142, 230–231, 295–296, 444, 457, 500, 509, 555, 596

Demas 515, 544, 551

Demons
general 435, 533, 647–648, 650
and Jesus 9, 19–21, 24, 31–32, 110–111, 188, 263, 268
(*see* Evil Spirits)

Derbe 342, 344, 347

Devil 6–7, 158–159, 277, 495, 532, 555, 598, 610, 621, 641–642, 654–655 (*see* Beelzebul, Satan)

Divorce 11, 12, 52–53, 118–119, 205, 427–428

Dorcas 329–330

Dragon 641–643, 647, 654

Drusilla 371

E

Egypt, flight to 4–5

Elders
Jewish 59, 73, 77, 79–81, 85, 313–314, 319, 370

Christian 335, 344–346, 360, 534–536, 546, 588, 598, 616, 618
heavenly 630–632, 634, 640, 652

Elijah 28, 46–47, 82, 148, 160, 238, 403, 589

Elisha 160

Elizabeth 147–150

Emmanuel *see* Immanuel

Emmaus 233

Emperor
title of Roman ruler 62, 126, 218
Augustus 151
Tiberius 156, 293
Claudius 335, 353
Nero 372–373, 506, 593–594

Epaphras 508, 515, 551

Ephesus,-ians 355–358, 360–361, 446, 448, 484, 529, 624–626

Epicureans 352

Esau 400, 572

Ethiopian 325–326

Eunice 539

Eutychus 359–360

Eve 466, 532

Evil Spirits 89, 96, 101–102, 116 (*see* Demons)

F

Faith
general 21, 48, 59, 206, 384, 388–389, 391, 457, 475–477, 570–574, 581, 584
in God 124–125, 276, 280, 389–391, 475, 570–574
in Christ 22–23, 91, 103, 237, 240, 243–244, 254, 266–267, 270–271, 299, 312, 350, 388–389, 402–403, 474–476, 611–615

False
messiahs 67–68, 131
prophets 17, 67–68, 131, 338, 602, 611–612, 627, 653–655

Fast,-ing
general 93, 154, 209
Day of Atonement 376

Jesus' teaching 15, 22, 93-94, 164-165
Christian 338, 344
Father, title of God 13-16, 18, 29-30, 65, 135, 156, 193, 230-231, 237, 249-251, 268-269, 280-288, 397, 478, 575, 609-610
Felix 369-372
Festival(s)
Passover 73-74, 80, 132-133, 140, 155, 222-223, 241-242, 248, 251, 273-274, 276, 279, 293, 336, 425, 573
Unleavened Bread 74, 132-133, 222, 335, 359
Pentecost (Harvest) 307, 360, 448-449
Shelters 257-258
New Moon 512
Dedication of Temple 268
unspecified 248
Festus 372-376
Forgive,-ness
general 14-15, 21, 51-52, 99, 125, 156, 171-173, 206, 299, 453, 492, 509, 511, 567, 607
no forgiveness 32, 97, 567

G

Gabriel 147-149
Galatia,-ns 347, 355, 471, 570
Galilee
Lake 8, 20-21, 34, 40, 43, 88, 92, 95-97, 101-102, 107-108, 161-162, 251, 253, 299-301 (*see* Lake Tiberias, Lake Gennesaret)
province 8-9, 52, 85, 88-89, 91, 154, 159, 239, 248, 256
Gallio 354
Gamaliel 317-318, 365
Genealogy
general 529
of Jesus 1-2, 157-158
Gennesaret *see* Lake Galilee
Gethsemane 76-77, 135-137
Gideon 574
Golgotha 81, 141, 294
Gomorrah 25, 401, 621
Greece,-k 258, 274, 294

H

Hades 205, 633
Hagar 479-480
Harvest Festival *see* Festival (Pentecost)
Heaven(s)
abode of God, angels, and blessed dead 6, 10, 14-15, 49, 54, 63, 84-85, 153, 184, 201, 225, 240, 243, 254-255, 312, 323, 384, 402, 447, 468, 495, 504, 508-509, 521, 525, 567, 576, 591, 596, 630-632, 652-653, 655-656
Kingdom of 5, 8, 9-11, 17-19, 24, 28, 34-38, 45, 49, 51, 53-55, 61, 65, 70
Father in 10, 13-14, 17-18, 34, 45, 49-51, 65
Hell 11, 26, 29, 49, 65-66, 118, 184, 191, 585, 602
Helper 281, 284
Herod
the Great, king of Judea 3-5, 147
Antipas, tetrarch of Galilee 38-39, 105-106, 113, 156-157, 178, 198, 228, 314, 338
Agrippa I 335-338
Agrippa II 372-376
Herodias 38, 105-106, 157
Hezekiah 2
High Priest
Jewish 73, 77-78, 136-138, 226, 273, 289-290, 313, 316-317, 319, 356, 367, 370, 563, 565-567, 577
Christ 555, 558-559, 562-564
Holy Spirit
in life and teaching of Jesus 2, 6, 31-32, 88, 149, 159, 184, 239, 245, 281, 284, 299, 305
in early church 307-310, 315-317, 325-326, 328-329, 331-335, 338, 342, 356
in letters of Paul 396-398, 438-439, 481-482
Husband(s)
literal 427-428, 494, 513, 594-595
figurative 466, 480, 655

I

Iconium 342, 344, 347, 542
Idol(s) 322, 352, 430-431,
433-435, 459, 517, 615, 627
Immanuel 3
Isaac 2, 19, 320, 400, 480, 572,
584
Isaiah 5, 8, 19, 31, 41, 87, 156,
159, 238, 276, 326, 381, 401,
403, 412
Israel 24, 43, 81, 142, 151, 154,
233, 238, 305, 317-318,
339-340, 400-406, 564, 634,
656
Italy,-ian 353, 376-380, 579

J

Jacob 2, 19, 149, 245-246, 320,
322, 400, 572
Jairus 103-104, 176-178
James
son of Zebedee 8, 46, 89, 103,
120-121, 130, 135, 162, 182,
306, 335
son of Alphaeus 24, 96, 166,
306
son of Mary 83, 142-143, 232
brother of Jesus 38, 104, 337,
345, 363, 473-474
father of Judas 166, 306
author of the letter 580
brother of Jude 620
Jeremiah 5, 45, 79
Jericho 57, 121, 185, 211-212,
573
Jerusalem
the city 3, 56-58, 67, 120,
122-123, 125, 153-155, 198,
213-216, 221, 241, 246, 248,
274, 305-306, 344-347
the heavenly 480, 576, 629,
655-657
Jesse 2, 339, 412
Jesus Christ
name 2-3, 149, 153
geneology 1-2, 157-158
birth and infancy 2-5,
148-149, 151-155
twelve years old 155-156
baptism and temptation 6-7,
88, 157-159
ministry in Galilee 8-52,
88-118, 159-182

Sermon on the Mount 9-18,
166-169
confession at Caesarea Philippi
45-46, 113-115, 179-180
transfiguration 46-47, 115,
180
last days in Jerusalem 57-84,
122-143, 213-232, 274-297
triumph'al entry 57-58,
122-123, 213-216, 274
in the Temple 59, 123-124,
216
discourse on last things
67-73, 129-132, 220-222
last supper 74-75, 133-134,
222-225, 276-288, 437-438
Gethsemane 76-77, 135-136,
225
arrest, trial, crucifixion, death,
burial 77-84, 136-143,
225-232, 288-297
resurrection, appearances, ascension 84-85, 143-145,
232-235, 305, 444
John
the Baptist 5-6, 27-28,
38-39, 60, 87-88, 105-106,
125, 147-148, 150-151,
156-157, 170-171, 187,
237-239, 244
son of Zebedee 8, 89, 104,
115, 117, 120-121, 130, 182,
222, 310-314, 325, 474
author of Revelation 623-
624, 658-659
father of Simon Peter 45,
239, 302
Mark 337-339, 347, 514, 544,
551, 599
of family of high priest Annas
313
Jonah 33, 44, 189
Joppa 329-332, 334
Jordan 5-6, 88, 118, 156, 238,
269
Joseph
son of Jacob 245, 320
husband of Mary 2-5, 148,
151-155, 240, 254
brother of Jesus 38, 104
brother of James "the youn-
ger" 83, 142-143

of Arimathea 83, 142–143, 231–232, 296–297
Barsabbas 306
Barnabas 315
Judas
Iscariot 74–75, 77, 79, 133, 136, 222, 225, 256, 273, 277–279, 288, 307
brother of Jesus 38, 104
apostle 281
the Galilean 318
of Damascus 328
Barsabbas, of Jerusalem 346–347
Jude 620
Judea 3, 5, 52, 68, 150, 244, 256, 270, 362, 413, 473, 518
Judge,-ment
Christ as Judge 250, 261, 267, 276, 333, 457, 543–544, 653
God as Judge 16, 168, 244, 385–386, 410, 570, 576, 584–585, 587, 644, 655
Day of Judgment 25, 29, 32–33, 184, 189, 250, 371, 602, 604–605

K

King
God 12, 531, 646
Christ 72–73, 214, 274, 290–291, 649, 653
"King of the Jews" (as title of Christ) 3, 79, 81, 139–141, 230, 290–292, 294
"King of Israel" (as title of Christ) 81, 142, 240, 274
King of Egypt, and Joseph 320–321

L

Lake Galilee 8, 20–21, 34, 40, 43, 88, 92, 95–97, 101, 107–108, also called Lake Tiberias 251, also called Lake Gennesaret 161
Lake Tiberias see Lake Galilee
Lamb
Festival of Passover 133, 222
figure or title of Christ 161

238–239, 425, 592, 631–635, 642, 649, 652–653, 656–658
Laodicea 510, 515, 629–630
Lazarus
of parable 205
from Bethany 270–274
Leper, Leprosy see Skin Diseases
Levi, apostle (also called Matthew) 92–93, 164
Levite,-ical 185, 238, 315
Lord's Prayer 14–15, 187
Lord's Supper 74–75, 133–134, 222–223, 437–438
Love
of God 244, 281, 285, 391, 399, 485, 487, 610, 612–613
of Christ 270, 277, 279, 282, 399, 457, 475, 489, 492, 624
Luke 515, 544, 551
Lydia 348, 350
Lysias, Claudias 369–371
Lystra 342–344, 347, 542

M

Macedonia 348, 357–359, 413, 448, 453, 460–461, 463, 466, 505, 517, 520, 529
"Magnificat" 149–150
Manna 254–255, 565, 627
Mark, John 337–339, 347, 514, 544, 551, 599
Martha 186–187, 270–273
Mary
mother of Jesus 2–5, 38, 104, 148–150, 152–156, 174, 240–241, 295, 306
Magdalene 83–84, 142–144, 173, 232, 295, 297–298
sister of Martha, of Bethany 186–187, 270–273
mother of John Mark 337
wife of Clopas, mother of James and Joseph 83–84, 142–143, 232, 295
Matthew 21, 96, 166 (see Levi)
Matthias 306–307
Melchizedek 559, 561–563
Mercy,-iful
God 150–151, 167, 400–401, 403–404, 406, 487, 529–531, 548, 590, 593

Christ 23, 42, 47–48, 57, 555, 622
Michael 621, 641
Midian 321
Miracles and Cures of Jesus
general references 8–9, 18–24, 30–31, 39–44, 53, 59, 89–92, 94–96, 101–104, 106–108, 161–164, 166, 170, 175–181, 240–243, 248–249, 251–254, 276, 299, 333
driving out demons
blind and dumb 31
daughter of woman of Tyre 42–43, 110–111
dumb man 24, 188
epileptic boy 47–48, 116, 180–181
Gerasene men 101–102, 175–176
man in Capernaum 89, 160–161
Mary Magdalene 143–144, 173
men of Gadara 20–21
woman in synagogue 196–197
other cures
blind Bartimaeus 121–122, 211–212
blind man at Bethsaida 113
man born blind 264–266
two blind men 23
deaf-mute 111
man with skin disease 18, 91, 162–163
man with crippled hand 30–31, 94–95, 165–166
man with swollen arms and legs 198
officer's servant 19, 169–170
paralyzed man in Capernaum 21, 91–92, 163–164
paralyzed man in Jerusalem 248–249
Peter's mother-in-law 19, 90, 161
slave of High Priest 226
son of official 248

ten men with skin disease 206–207
woman with severe bleeding 22, 103, 176–177
raising of dead
daughter of Jairus 22–23, 103–104, 176–178
son of widow of Nain 170
Lazarus 270–272
other miracles
coin in fish's mouth 48
cursing the fig tree 59, 123
feeding the five thousand 39–40, 106–107, 178–179, 251–253
feeding the four thousand 43–44, 111–112
great catch of fish 161–162
another great catch of fish 299–302
stilling the storm 20, 101, 175
walking on the water 40, 107–108, 253
water changed to wine 240–241
Miracles and Cures by Others
the apostles 24–25, 104–105, 178, 316
the seventy-two 183–184
Philip 324–325
Peter 310–311, 329–330
Paul 338–339, 343–344, 348, 469
Moses
person 18, 47, 53, 127, 205, 218, 243, 251, 266, 319–322, 400, 402–403, 454–455, 555–557, 573, 621, 646
Law of, book of 127, 153, 235, 237, 240, 319, 341, 345, 381, 455
Mount of Olives 57, 67, 75, 122, 130, 134, 213–214, 222, 225, 259, 306

N

Naaman 160
Nain 170
Nathanael 240, 299

Nazarene
  title of Jesus 5
  name of believers 370
Nazareth 5, 38, 58, 88-89, 104, 138, 151, 154, 159-160, 240
New Moon Festival see Festival
Nicodemus 243-244, 259, 297
Nicolaitans 625, 627
Nineveh 33, 189
Noah 69, 208, 571, 596, 602
"Nunc Dimittis" 154

O

Obey, Obedience, Obedient
  to God or Christ 89, 101, 244-245, 317, 559, 613
  to demand of gospel 394, 453, 461, 500, 525, 527
  to human beings 317, 408-409, 494-495, 547, 593-595
Onesimus 514, 550-551

P

Pamphylia 307, 339, 344, 347, 376
Parables
  reason and use 34-36, 98-99, 173-174
  told by Jesus
    children sitting 28, 171
    faithful servant 70, 194-195
    fig tree 69, 131, 221-222
    friend at midnight 187
    gold coins 212-213
    good Samaritan 185-186
    great feast 199-200
    hidden treasure 37
    home owner 37-38
    king going to war 200
    lamp under a bowl 10, 99, 174, 189
    lost coin 201
    lost sheep 49-50, 201
    lost son 201-203
    mustard seed 36, 100-101, 197
    net 37
    new patch 22, 94, 165

    pearl 37
    Pharisee and tax collector 209
    places at wedding feast 199
    rich fool 192
    rich man and Lazarus 205
    seed growing 97-98, 100
    servant 206
    shrewd manager 203-204
    sower 34-35, 97-99, 173-174
    ten girls 70-71
    tenants in vineyard 60-61, 125-126, 217
    three servants 71-72
    tower building 200
    two debtors 172
    two house builders 18, 169
    two sons 60
    unforgiving servant 51-52
    unfruitful fig tree 196
    watchful home owner 69-70, 194
    watchful servants 132, 194
    wedding feast 61-62
    wedding guests 22, 94, 165
    weeds 35-37
    widow and judge 208-209
    wine and wineskins 22, 94, 165
    workers in vineyard 55-56
    yeast 36, 197
Paradise 230, 468
Passover see Festival
Patmos 624
Paul
  early life
    born in Tarsus 365
    sister 368
    educated in Jerusalem under Gamaliel 365
    tent maker by trade 353-354
    approved of Stephen's death 324, 366
    persecuted Christians 324, 365, 374, see also 444, 472, 502, 531
  conversion 327-328, 366, 374-375
  early ministry
    Arabia 473

Damascus 328-329, 375, 468, 473
Jerusalem 329, 338, 375, 472-473
Tarsus 329
Antioch 334-335, 338, 344
missionary activity
first tour 338-344
Jerusalem council 344-347
second tour 347-355
third tour 355-361
return to Jerusalem 361-363
arrest and imprisonment
arrest in Jerusalem 364-369
imprisonment and trial in Caesarea 369-376
voyage to Rome 376-380
ministry in Rome 380-381
letters
Colossians 507-515
1 Corinthians 416-449
2 Corinthians 450-470
Ephesians 484-496
Galatians 471-483
Philemon 549-551
Philippians 497-506
Romans 382-415
1 Thessalonians 516-523
2 Thessalonians 524-528
1 Timothy 529-537
2 Timothy 538-544
Titus 545-548
Peace
from God 152, 154, 391, 413, 470, 498, 505, 507, 509
from Christ 281, 286, 488, 498, 513, 528
Pentecost see Festival
Pergamum 626-627
Peter
call to be disciple 8, 88-89, 161-162, 239
declaration about Jesus 45-46, 113-114, 179, 256
on Mount of Transfiguration 46-47, 115, 180, 601
in Garden of Gethsemane 76-77, 135-136, 225, 288-289
denies Jesus 78-79, 138-139, 226-227, 289

sees risen Lord 234-235, 299-303, 444
sermon at Pentecost 307-310
activity in Jerusalem, Judea, and Samaria 310-318, 325, 329-337, 345
dispute with Paul at Antioch 474
prediction of his death 302
letters
1 Peter 590-599
2 Peter 600-605
Pharisee(s) 5-6, 21-22, 24, 30-33, 41, 44-45, 53, 62-66, 83, 171-173, 204, 209, 238, 243, 245, 258-259, 345, 368, 374
Philadelphia 628-629
Philip
apostle 24, 239-240, 251-252, 274-275, 280
helper and evangelist 318, 324-326, 362
ruler 156
first husband of Herodias 38, 105
Philippi 348-350, 359, 497, 517
Phoebe 413
Pilate 79-80, 139-140, 156, 195, 227-229, 290-294, 312, 314, 340, 537
Prayer(s)
teaching of Jesus 13-15, 187, 208-209
in life of Jesus 40, 76-77, 90, 107, 134-136, 157, 163, 166, 179-180, 187, 223-225, 286-288, 559
teaching in the Letters 398, 442, 496, 505, 514, 523, 531-532, 588-589, 614, 622
Priscilla 353-355, 413-414, 449, 544
Prophet(s),-ess
of Old Testament 2-5, 8, 28, 66-67, 198, 308-309, 312, 326, 383, 552, 591
of New Testament 338, 440, 490, 639-640, 651, 658
Agabus 335, 362
Anna 154
Christian 335, 338, 346-347, 440, 490, 651-652, 658

Jesus 38, 58, 61, 105, 170, 172, 198, 233, 246, 248, 265
John the Baptist 27–28, 38–39, 60, 125, 150, 160, 171, 216
Judas and Silas 346–347
"the Prophet" 238, 252, 259, 312
the two witnesses 639–640

Q

Quirinius 151

R

Rachel 5
Rahab 2, 573, 584
Rebecca 400
Red Sea 321, 433, 573
Resurrection
interpretation of Jesus' resurrection 309, 317, 333, 340, 383, 393–394, 444–446 (see Jesus Christ)
of men 250, 254–255, 368, 444–448
daughter of Jairus 22–23, 103–104, 176–178
son of widow of Nain 170
Lazarus 270–272
Dorcas 329–330
Rhoda 337
Rome 307, 353, 357, 368, 380, 383, 539

S

Sadducees 5, 44–45, 63, 127, 218, 313, 316, 368
Salome 142–143
Samaria 206, 245, 305, 324–325, 345
Samaritan(s)
Samaritans who would not receive Jesus 182
parable of the good Samaritan 185–186
men with skin disease 206–207
Samaritan woman 245–248
Samson 574
Sapphira 315–316

Sarah 390, 400, 572, 594–595
Sardis 628
Satan 7, 32, 46, 88, 97, 99, 114, 184, 188, 222, 224, 279, 315, 415, 424, 427, 467, 526, 531, 626–628, 641–642, 654 (see Beelzebul, Devil)
Saul
king of Israel 339
apostle Paul 324, 326–329, 335, 338 (see Paul)
Savior
God 147, 529, 531, 534, 547–548, 622
Christ 152, 248, 317, 339–340, 494, 504, 539, 546–547, 600–601, 603–605, 612
Sergius Paulus 338
Sermon on the Mount 9–18, 166–169
Sharon 329
Shelters, Festival of see Festival
Sidon 29, 42, 111, 160, 184, 337, 376
Silas 346–351, 354, 452, 516, 524, 598
Siloam 196, 265
Simeon 154
Simon
Peter see Peter
the patriot 24, 96, 166, 306
brother of Jesus 38, 104
of Bethany 74, 132
from Cyrene 81, 141, 229
Pharisee 171–173
father of Judas Iscariot 256, 277, 279
the magician, of Samaria 324–325
the leatherworker, of Joppa 330–332
Skin Disease 18, 74, 91, 132, 160, 162–163, 206–207
Smyrna 626
Sodom 25, 29, 184, 208, 401, 602, 621, 639
Solomon 2, 16, 33, 189, 193, 322
Solomon's Porch 268, 311, 316

Son: titles of Jesus
  Son of Man 20-21, 25, 28, 30,
    32-33, 37, 45-48, 55-57,
    68-70, 72-73, 75, 77-78, 209,
    240, 243, 250, 253, 255, 261,
    266, 275, 279, 323
  Son of God 6-7, 20, 40, 45,
    47, 78, 81, 83, 87-88, 142,
    149, 239-240, 244, 250,
    269-271, 293, 299, 328, 383,
    391, 396-399, 417, 475, 478,
    490, 517, 553, 558-560, 569,
    609, 612, 614-615
  Son of David 1, 23, 31, 42,
    58-59, 64, 101-102, 116
Spirit, Holy *see* Holy Spirit
Spirit(s), unclean or evil 89,
  96-97
Stephen 318-324, 366
Stoics 352
Syria,-n 8, 151, 160, 346-347,
  355, 358, 362, 473

T

Tabernacle *see* Tent
Tabernacle, Festival of *see*
  Festival, Shelters
Tabitha 329-330
Tarsus 329, 335, 365
Tax
  general 48, 62-63, 126,
    217-218
  collector(s) 21, 28, 60, 92-93,
    157, 164, 171, 201, 209, 212
Temple
  in Jerusalem 7, 59, 67, 77-79,
    81-82, 123-125, 129-130,
    142, 147-148, 153-155, 216,
    220, 235, 241-242, 257-258,
    261, 268, 310-311, 316-317,
    364
  figurative 242, 422, 459, 488
Tent, figurative 456-457, 563,
  565-567, 646
**Tent of the LORD's Presence,
  Covenant Tent, Israelite cen-
  ter of worship before Temple
  was built** 322, 565-567
Tertius 415
Tertullus 370
Thaddaeus 24, 96

Thessalonica,-ns 350-351, 505,
  516, 524
Thomas 24, 96, 166, 270, 280,
  299, 306
Thousand Years 604, 654
Thyatira 348, 627-628
Tiberias
  lake *see* Lake Galilee
  town 253
Tiberius 156
Timothy 347, 351, 354, 357,
  359, 415, 424, 449-450, 452,
  497, 501, 507, 516, 519, 524,
  529, 531, 537-538, 549, 579
Titus 453, 460-463, 469, 473,
  544-545
Tongues (speaking in tongues)
  307, 333, 356, 439-440
Troas 348, 359-360, 453, 544
Tychicus 359, 496, 514, 544,
  548
Tyre 29, 42, 110-111, 166, 184,
  337, 362

U

Unleavened Bread *see* Festival

V

Vine 282, 646
Vineyard 55-56, 60-61,
  125-126, 217, 646
Virgin 2-3, 149, 429, 466

W

Widow(s) 128-129, 170,
  208-209, 220, 318, 330, 427,
  534-535
Wife,-ves 427-430, 494, 513,
  594-595
Wine
  literal 22, 81, 94, 141-142,
    148, 165, 185, 240-241, 411,
    493, 532, 536
  figurative 644, 648, 650
Winged Creatures 565
Wrath of God 245, 384, 386,
  391, 401, 408, 487, 492, 512,
  519, 633-634, 644, 646-647

Y

Yes 12, 451–452
Yoke 30

Z

Zacchaeus 212

Zebedee 8, 56, 83, 89, 120, 162, 299
Zechariah, father of John the Baptist 147–151
Zion
  term for Jerusalem in entirety 58, 274, 402, 406
  heavenly Jerusalem 576, 644

MAPS

PALESTINE IN THE TIME OF JESUS

Miles 0 — 40
Kms 0 — 40

Sidon
Zarephath
MT. HERMON
Abila
ABILENE
Damascus
SYRIA
LEBANON MTS.
Tyre
Caesarea Philippi
PHOENICIA
MEDITERRANEAN
SEA
Ptolemais
GALILEE
Chorazin
Capernaum
Bethsaida
Magadan
Lake
Galilee
MT. CARMEL
Cana
Tiberias
Nazareth
Nain
MT. TABOR
Gadara
Caesarea
TEN TOWNS
(Decapolis)
Salim
SAMARIA
Aenon
Gerasa
Samaria
MT. EBAL
MT. GERIZIM
Sychar
Joppa
Jordan River
PEREA
Arimathea?
Ephraim
Emmaus
Jerusalem
Bethany
Azotus
Bethany
Qumran
Ascalon
Bethlehem
JUDEA
Gaza
Hebron
Dead
Sea
IDUMEA
NABATEA

THE WORLD OF THE
NEW TESTAMENT

0   Miles   300

0   Kms   300

© United Bible Societies, 1977

JERUSALEM IN NEW TESTAMENT TIMES

Yards 0 — 400
Meters 0 — 400

━━━ Walls in the time of Jesus
═══ Later walls built by Agrippa I

Road to Caesarea

Early wall of unknown origin and date

Road to Joppa

Pool of Bethzatha

Antonia Fortress (Praetorium?)

Sheep Gate

TEMPLE

Solomon's Porch

Portico

Golgotha

Pool

Bridge

Royal Portico

Stair-case

Street

Hasmonean Palace

Hippodrome

Herod's Palace

Herodian Street

Theater?

Aqueduct

Pool

?

Pool of Siloam

Gihon Spring

Tunnel

Gethsemane

To Mount of Olives

Tombs

Road to Jericho

Road to Bethany

Kidron Valley

Hinnom Valley

Enrogel Spring

Road to Bethlehem

Road to the Dead Sea

© United Bible Societies, 1976